Grandma Talks Tech: Baby Boomers Take To iPads, Too!

BY

SHEILA "GRANDMA" GRIFFITH

See What Readers Are Saying!

"... an in-depth book to help seniors learn their iPad presented in an easy to read and understand way. The author's extensive teaching experience with this subject matter really comes through...This book is a must have addition to enhance with your iPad experience."
EP

"Whether you are considering buying an iPad, or already have one, you could not get better instruction than with GRANDMA TALKS TECH; BABY BOOMERS TAKE TO IPADS, TOO!..."

"...There is so much to know, and Griffith clearly breaks the large pieces into smaller, digestible chunks such as Keyboard Shortcuts and an overview of Settings from Top to Bottom..."

"...There is something for every interest -- from working with iTunes to fine tuning your calendar to working with Photos and FaceTime -- each section filled with clear, concise explanations..."

"...If the iPad can do it, Griffith can tell you how to proceed to get the most value and enjoyment from your tablet. This is one savvy grandma. Highly Recommended."
BF

"Like many good books, it takes a subject which intimidates the iPad and e reader user and is clear and direct about its functions and how to do it. You feel more confident after reviewing Grandma talks tech. I keep a copy on my iPad for easy and quick access. Sheila Griffith knows how to clarify the technical side of what has become a standard, the iPad in a digital age. Would highly recommend this book."
MVR

Table of Contents

Part Two - Built-In Apps

Part Three - iPad Third Generation and Later

Part Four - Tips and Tricks

Part Five - Covering Your Apps

Part Six - What to Do If Your iPad Gets Quirky

Part Seven - Peripherals

Part Eight - Appendices

To George, the love of my life

without whom I wouldn't be whole -

even with all my gadgets

Acknowledgements

Before beginning this journey into one of the most amazing little gadgets I've had the pleasure of working with, I'd like to thank my loving husband, George (whom I hope forgives me for my portrayal of him in this book; in reality, he's an angel and I couldn't do without him); my terrific children, George and Tracie; their spouses, Gena and Scott; my eleven (11) wonderful grandchildren, Niome, Michael, Brianna, Joey, Alex, Joshua, Nathan, Sarah, Haileigh, Timothy and Matthew; and, of course, my two dear great-granddaughters Jubilee and Jamie They have all given me support through this process of pouring my heart and soul into a project. I never could have done this without them. I'd also like to thank a very special person to whom I owe a debt of gratitude, my close friend LaTosha Young. Her feedback was invaluable and much appreciated. A special thank you goes out to Barney Slice whose wonderful cartoon logo art was indispensable. Finally, a warm and appreciative thank you is sent to all my former students, and particularly to Martha, for their fresh and special perspectives, all of whom have contributed to this book in one way or another by inspiring me to begin this project. The inspiration I've felt stems from their inquisitiveness and desire to conquer new technology, by hook or by crook. This book is dedicated to all of the special people involved; and in memory of a very special person whose recent death affected me deeply and changed my life in a way that enabled me to write this book, Eileen Schoenig.

Introduction

I have been involved with computers of one sort or another since the early days of basic computers in 1973. They have been not only my vocation but my avocation. As far back as I can remember, I have been the "go-to" person when a computer was "acting up."

In the early 80's, I began taking college coursework in the field, eventually studying and becoming a web developer. I've always embraced new technologies, always being one of the first to adopt them and, as such, always paying the most for them (but that's another subject I won't go into here). My husband might be listening!

I remember well, the early Atari and Commodore computers. Mobile technology has been no different. As a matter of fact, if anything, I've spent more time with my mobile devices and gadgets, if that's possible. I owned one of the first Blackberry devices in their early years when there was a question of whether this Canadian firm would survive and be a player in the market. I owned the first iPhone shortly after it was released; I owned the first iPod; and one of the early Android devices. As you can see, I'm quite addicted.

In recent years, my husband opened a business in our local area, The Write Solutions LLC d/b/a Grandma Talks Tech. In it, we do web design, computer training (both PC and Mac), and, of course, iPad and Android training. We do both private lessons and also teach Baby Boomers and other seniors at a local University OLLI program. We have been retired now for quite a few years and enjoy our small business which keeps us busy and definitely prevents boredom from setting in.

One of the first things I like to convey to my students, and I'd like you to know, is there is very little you can do on your iPad that can't be undone, sometimes easily, sometimes not so (but I've never lost a patient yet, to coin a phrase). I'll try to remind you of this frequently throughout this book because it is an important lesson to learn.

You may have marveled at the way in which small children can adapt to iPads and other electronics, but I attribute this to two very important factors. First, they've grown up with these technologies, just like we grew up with TV and remote controls (men especially have mastered their use since an early age). No offense men, just saying. The second and equally as important reason is they have no earthly idea how many work hours, and related stress and hard work, went into purchasing them. They have absolutely no fear of them because, if they break it, there'll be more. Baby Boomers, on the other hand, know exactly how hard it was to earn the money required to buy one of these gadgets and, let's face it, they're not cheap. Is it any wonder we fear that we'll do damage to it in some way if it's not handled exactly right?!

Now that I've given you my background information and this important information to remember about iPad use as we work our way through this book, we're ready to begin. We'll start at the beginning: By getting to know your iPad. Even if you're a little more experienced iPad user, you may find something in Chapter 1 that you didn't know. Some of you more advanced users may wish to skip ahead a little to Part 2 or the chapter on iOS 6.x. If so, feel free to do so. For you uninitiated, let's get started…

NOTE: This book primarily discusses iOS 6.0, but iOS 6.1 really introduced only one notable change for iPad users. With iOS 6.1, Siri (on iPad Third Generation or later) was also capable of obtaining movie tickets at many local movie theaters; other than that, the only other major change dealt with LTE capabilities primarily for iPhone wireless reception. As of this revision, iOS 6.1.1 was already a reality patching any holes that jailbreaking software manufacturer's had opened with their iOS 6.1 jailbreaking software for iPads and iPhones, among other things.

PART ONE
Navigating Your iPad

CHAPTER 1

Getting to Know Your iPad

Before we begin our trek of getting to know your iPad, we actually have to "Get to know our iPad." That being the case, we'll start with the basics. The first thing anyone will need to know is the Sleep/Wake button. As you might guess, the Sleep/Wake button, located on the top right, not only puts your iPad to sleep and wakes it, but it also turns it on and off. How many of you have turned your iPad off or on? This might be a trick question, so think about it for a minute. The answer is, unless you've held that button down until the "Power Off" slider comes up, you have only put it to sleep. To actually turn it off, you need to, not only hold it down until you get the slider, but actually touch and slide it to the right until it "Powers off." To turn it back on, you press and hold it again until the apple appears.

Go ahead, try it now! You don't have to actually turn it off unless you want to, but check out the function. Press and hold the Sleep/Wake button until that power off slider comes up so you can see what I mean.

If you turn it off, just come back to this book and we'll pick up where we left off. Now if I ask how many of you have turned your iPad off and on, I'll bet I get a lot more correct answers, if my classes have been any indication.

Next, let's look at the Home button The Home button is on the front bottom of your iPad, right in the middle. This button will also put your iPad to sleep and wake it, in addition to taking you to your Home Screen. By your Home Screen, I mean the opening screen with the built in application (app) icons, if you haven't rearranged your icons yet. We'll be talking about that later in this book but, for now, just know that this button will take you to your Opening Screen. Now, if you have more than one app open, you can "Double Tap" that button and multi-task. You'll see a double window open with the top section being the app you were just working in and the bottom being a "Scrollable" section of icons representing all the other open apps on your iPad. You can choose any of those icons to go to a second app and multi-task. This was a new feature of iOS 5.0. If you haven't yet upgraded to iOS 5.0, we'll be going over upgrading to iOS 6.x and onward in the next chapter. If you're not sure what operating system you have on your iPad at present, go to Settings -> General -> About and look about halfway down the page for "Version." If it says 5.1.1, you'll need to update. If you haven't updated to iOS 6.x, but you're still in iOS 5.0 or better, the features we'll be discussing will be available to you now. If, as I say, you're below 5.0, we'll help you upgrade in the next chapter.

So, getting back to the Home button, another neat thing you can do with this button is tap and hold it briefly along with the Sleep/Wake button, that we just talked about, to take a screenshot of your iPad. You may wonder why you would want to take a picture of your screen, but there are several very good reasons for doing so. For example, if you were having a problem with your iPad, or even an app on it, tech support might request a copy of a screen shot so they could "see" what's happening and ascertain the possible cause or causes. Of course, if it weren't for screen shots, I wouldn't be able to show you all the illustrations I hope to show you in this book. That alone is reason enough to have this built in functionality, IMHO (In My Humble Opinion, see Messaging Shortcuts in Glossary)!

With iOS 6.0 and greater and the iPad 3 or later, holding this Home button will also awaken Siri, your onboard personal assistant. We'll discuss her in more detail in a section of her own.

Next, we'll discuss the "Mute" button. The Mute button is a little slider switch on the upper right side of your iPad. The default setting is for that switch to be a Mute button. It doesn't mute all sounds but will mute most sounds from your iPad. To mute sounds, slide the switch down. If you choose, you can instead set this button to be a screen rotation lock switch. If, for example, you're working on a paper that keeps flipping from Landscape to Portrait view and is driving you absolutely crazy, with the lock rotation setting enabled, you would only need to slide the switch down once the screen was in your preferred mode and it would remain that way until you unlocked it. You can't have it both ways, though. It can either be used as a mute switch or a rotation lock switch, but not both at the same time! To enable the lock rotation mode, go to Settings -> General -> Use Side Switch To and enable Lock Rotation. Should you want to go back to using it as a Mute switch at any time, just go back and enable Mute. You can use the setting as often as you wish if you have a preference for various tasks; however, you'll have to make your adjustments the same way by going back to Settings each time.

There is another way to lock rotation that we'll discuss a little later on in this book but, for now, let's just cover the physical make-up of the iPad itself which brings us next to the volume controls. The volume controls are located immediately below the mute switch. They're fairly intuitive, like most Apple "i" devices, once you get used to them. You press and hold the upper control to turn the volume up and press and hold the bottom control to turn the sound down.

The Dock Connector is next and is located at the bottom of your device. This is where you connect the charging cable. This is a pretty versatile feature, as you'll learn later, since it can be used for much more than just syncing and charging your iPad.

And, the last physical feature I want to point out to you is the audio jack which is on the top left side of your iPad when you hold it in portrait mode with the Dock Connector on the bottom. It is a little opening that you use to plug in headsets, some speakers, and some styli. Yes, that's right, I use mine for styli transporting. Sometimes it is much easier for me to use a capacitive screen stylus, along with hand gestures as needed, so I find it most convenient to cart along my favorite stylus by plugging it into the audio jack by the connecting string that some styli come with. I know it should have a much more technical name than that but, if there is, it escapes me and I call it just a connecting string. It is usually black with a metal plug on the end that fits through the hole in the top of the stylus and loops around so it doesn't come off. It's that little metal plug that fits perfectly into the audio jack and does no harm to any internal components as it doesn't fit that far into the opening. You can find these styli in any office supply store or, at our online store, at http:// GrandmaTalksTech.com. Just do a search for stylus and you're bound to see one or two with just such a connector. My favorite is the rooCASE Stylus for capacitive screens but there are many excellent ones on the market today.

Accessibility

The iPad's Helping Hand

Before we go any further, I want to point out some iPad features that may help some of us really navigate our iPads. Not all iPad owners are fortunate enough to be able to utilize these wonderful devices to their fullest due to disabilities of one form or another. Apple has anticipated this and designed the iPad to be assistive in as many ways as possible. We'll discuss some of those ways here.

Vision Problems

Many people, especially as we age, develop visual handicaps of some form. To address this, Apple has included several features, especially in the new iPad Third Generation and later. Beginning with the third generation model, with iOS 6.0 not only is there a dictation feature, but as you'll see later in this book, also has Siri, to assist with many iPad functions. Siri can do many things that, prior to iOS 6.0 had to be done by hand. I recommend you also see the chapter on Siri and dictation later in this book for specifics. Many of you probably know already that type on an iPad in Mail or Safari, for example, can be enlarged by "pinching out," which will be explained in the next chapter on gestures.

Additionally, there are settings in the Settings app that can be adjusted to suit your physical needs and personal taste.

If you go to Settings -> General -> Accessibility -> Vision, you'll see a number of settings there specifically for the visually impaired. Settings include: VoiceOver, Zoom, Large Text, Invert Colors, Speak Selection, and Speak Auto-Text. Personally, I always have "Speak Selection" and "Speak Auto-text" enabled. I don't use them all the time, but there are certainly times when I find them irreplaceable.

If you have any difficulties seeing, I highly recommend you go to this section before we even get started with this book. You may have to play around with the settings a little bit to tweak them and get them "just right" but, once set, you should not have to adjust them again. You'll find your enjoyment of your iPad is dramatically improved when you can adjust it to accommodate your needs.

Just a note, don't forget to go to the bottom of the column and enable the Triple-click Home "VoiceOver" feature if you'd like additional assistance (see "Triple-Click Home" below).

Hearing

Many more of us, although I'm not sure of the numbers, develop hearing problems as we age. If you go to Settings -> General -> Accessibility -> Hearing, you'll see two settings that you can adjust there to assist in your use and enjoyment of your iPad. You can enable Mono Audio and/ or adjust the audio balance of your iPad speakers to favor one side over another.

Learning

If you are helping someone that is somehow developmentally impaired, you can enable "Guided Access." If you go to Settings -> General -> Accessibility -> Learning, you can tap the right facing arrow to turn "Guided Access" on by sliding the switch on the right to the "On" position where it will turn blue and say "On." Once this is done, you activate the feature by triple-clicking the Home button and following the instructions in whichever app you open. I have not tested this extensively to know if this feature will work with all App Store purchases, but it will definitely work with all of the iPad's built-in apps.

On-screen instructions will be provided for any native iPad app if this feature has been activated. The instructions will walk the user through every step of the way assisting the very young, the very old, and the other wise learning disabled user.

Physical & Motor

Motor skills can be another victim of age or disability. Going to Settings -> General -> Accessibility -> Physical & Motor to adjust those settings can be a big help. Here you can enable assistive touch where you set your own gestures to activate various features of your iPad. Another setting here will adjust the speed at which you must click the Home button for multi click features.

Triple-click Home

The final accessibility setting is the Triple-click setting. This setting adjusts the controls of a triple-click on the Home button. You can set a triple-click of the Home button to: Initiate VoiceOver, Invert Colors, Zoom, or enable the Assistive Touch feature.

This can be used in conjunction with any or all of the aforementioned accessibility settings.

CHAPTER 2

iOS Features

W hen it comes to mobile operating system features, iOS devices rank right up there at the top of the quality and performance spectrum. When I talk about mobile operating systems, iOS on iPads, iPod Touches, and iPhones, I'm referring to the mobile equivalent to Windows on a PC or OSX 10.7.3, Lion, on a Mac. Of course, the latest for the Mac is Mountain Lion, for Microsoft that would be Windows 8, for Android (another mobile operating system) it would be Jelly Bean, and for iOS it's 6.x. At the time of this writing, iOS 6.1 is brand new but iOS 5.x was not that old either.

Released in Fall 2011, iOS 5.0 introduced over 200 changes to Apple's previous mobile operating system. Well, don't get too comfortable with that iOS device yet, thinking you've finally mastered it, because the recent, Fall 2012, release of iOS 6.0 introduces another 200+!

In this book, we're going to go over all of the changes introduced over the last two major releases, updating those that changed from iOS 4.3 to 5.1.1, as well as introducing those changes that are brand new with the release of iOS 6.0 and 6.1. By the time you read this, who knows what release Apple may be on, as fast as technology changes today. But that's the subject of another whole book.

If you're a baby boomer, which I suspect many of you reading this today are, you may be scratching your head trying to figure out when iOS 4.3 changed, or even what it is, and saying "It seems like just yesterday..." and you'd certainly be correct. It wasn't much before yesterday, it's just a fact of life in the 21st century that technology changes as fast as you may change your underwear (sometimes faster).

As baby boomers, we're sometimes amazed at the speed at which our children and grandchildren pick up and adapt to these new technologies but, let's not forget they've been brought up with them. It's like taking a second breath for most of them. And, as for the grandchildren, they don't have the kind of money wrapped up in these things that the parents and grandparents do, so it's a lot easier to just go at it and relax completely in the handling of them. I say they don't have the kind of money wrapped up in them, but you know what I'm saying. Although the parents and grandparents have the money wrapped up in them, most young children have no concept of how much money it costs or how hard it is to make that money to afford it.

iOS 5.x

Moving on, as I say, iOS 5.x provided over 200 new features when it was introduced in Fall 2011. Some of those features were completely new additions, increasing the functionality of the devices and, in some cases, markedly so. iCloud, while not a physical change to the operating system, was a dramatic change in the ability of these marvelous devices. As many of you may still be trying to figure out iCloud, and what that entails, we'll be introducing it in more detail as this book progresses. Having the ability to back up to a cyber source and not use active hard drive space on your PC or Mac is a pretty wondrous thing. A lot of uncertainty remains for many as we, particularly baby boomers, are not entirely comfortable having all that information "out there" where just anyone might have access to it. Some of these concerns have a very real basis; some others may be laid to rest once you've heard a bit more about how it all works. For now, just think about the opportunity this feature provided when introduced.

Although cloud back-ups were not new nor conceptualized with Apple's introduction of them at that time, the whole idea of cloud back up was still pretty much unthought of by many, if not most, seniors. We all know Apple is a real innovator and they were even in this arena, offering iTools, MobileMe's precursor, which included iCloud type features with iDisk back in January 2000 which later became MobileMe, iCloud's forefather. By the time iCloud was introduced in Fall 2011, they were joining many others in the field including drop box, box. net, Sugarsync, and Amazon Cloud among them. Apple's iTools and MobileMe services were file hosting solutions for individuals back in the early days of what has become better known as "Cloud" services for corporate customers.

Among the benefits iCloud offered was FindMyiPhone which also works for iPad and iPod Touch. This feature was also a part of the earlier Apple MobileMe offering but, now that any iOS device (and Macs running OSX 10.7.x Lion and up) can access iCloud storage, it's a tough feature to overlook. If it's activated and your device is lost or stolen, FindMyiPhone can track it and show you on a map, within feet, where it is located. If you believe it's in the wrong person's hands, you can sound an alarm, have a message flash across the screen to the perpetrator or finder, password lock it, and/or wipe it clean so no one can access your information. You can do any one or as many of these things as you see fit, given the situation. Don't worry too much about the extreme of wiping it clean because, if it's later returned to you, and you've been backing up to iCloud or iTunes, as I'll show you in this book, you can always restore it from the back up and it'll be right back in the same condition it was in the last time you backed up.

Another nice feature that iOS 5.x introduced was PhotoStream. PhotoStream enabled syncing of photos from your iOS devices to each of your other iOS devices and your OSX 10.7.x Lion operated Mac. Other syncing, such as contact and calendar update syncing, would occur instantaneously if you were backing up all devices to iCloud. This was, and still is, pretty state of the art stuff. To update something on your iPad, then go to your iPhone or iPod Touch, and find the change has already been made there is pretty amazing, even in this day and age. So as not to confuse you, PhotoStream and other syncing are two different things but by comparison they are along the same lines.

Also introduced at that time were Notifications. For those users familiar with the Android operating system, this was not a new concept. Functioning in a very familiar way to many, Notifications were created in Settings for various apps. Accessing them was, and remains, just a matter of dragging down (as you'll learn to do in a minute) from the top center of your screen. Notifications would also appear as banner images on your Lock and Home screens.

Finally, AirPlay was also introduced. This technology enabled your iPad to connect wirelessly to your TV or Stereo Speakers, via an Apple TV module or AirPlay enabled speakers, respectively. With an AirPort Express component, you didn't even need the AirPlay enabled speakers, you could connect any speaker to the AirPort Express and play audio from your iPad anywhere throughout your home.

Gestures

We can't overlook one of the big changes with iOS devices that the introduction of iOS 5.x impacted: Gestures. There are several Gestures you'll become quite adept at as you become more and more familiar with your new or old device. The first of these that we'll discuss is the Flick. The Flick occurs when you touch the screen and rub your finger lightly against the screen up, down or, occasionally side-to-side, either right to left, or left to right. You do this to scroll through pages or lists. To stop the scrolling, you tap the screen or wait for the scroll to come to a rest, if you want to go through an entire list. An example of a time you would use this is when you have several contacts extending beyond the scope of the screen and want to get to a lower part of alphabet. Now, don't think that, if you have a number of contacts, this is the only way to get to the x, y, or z. You can always perform a search by entering the beginning letters and, the more letters entered, the more focused the choices will become. But, believe me when I tell you, there are many times you'll want or need to "Flick" the screen - and I'm not just talking about when you get annoyed with it!

The next gesture is the Drag. To "Drag," you put your finger on the screen, hold it lightly and move it around to display a web page, a map, or a page that is too large to display otherwise. Related to the "Drag," also introduced in 5.0 and included in subsequent versions, is the "Drag" from the very top of your screen downward. This gesture reveals the notifications screen. Notifications on your iPad are set up in "Settings" by individual apps. Not all apps have a notification feature, but those that do are listed in your Settings -> Notifications -> "AppName." Tap on the app name to set up the notifications for any particular app. An example of a notification would be a notice from "Reminders" or "Calendar" that you have an appointment. Generally speaking, when you receive a notification and are not using your iPad at the time, an alarm will sound (if you set it up that way), and a "Banner" will appear on your lock screen (the screen that has the slider on it and first appears when you go to your iPad after a period of non-use). Depending on how you set it up, if you're using your iPad when a notification is scheduled to appear, you may get a banner in the middle or top of your screen, with or without an alarm. Once shown, if you don't tap it right away to go to it, it'll go into that notifications page that you pull down, until you tap it to show it or delete it.

Next is the double-tap. You tap twice quickly on the screen to zoom in on maps, web pages, and pictures. You don't have to do this hard, and use the flesh of your finger tip, not the nail, if you can. Technically, you should be able to tap once to zoom out once the page is enlarged, but the tapping gesture takes patience, persistence, and just the right touch in my experience with new iPad users. Now don't give up completely if you can't get the tapping motion down right because you can always use the fall back gestures of "Pinching" and "Un-pinching." To enlarge or zoom into one of the fore-mentioned screens, "Un-pinch" using your forefinger and thumb and, do the opposite, or "Pinch" to zoom out. This gesture requires just two or three fingers. Some, as you'll soon see, require four or five fingers.

Before attempting the next few gestures, you need to go to Settings -> General -> Multitasking Gestures and enable or turn them on. Once you've done this, "Swipe" up with 4 or 5 fingers and you'll reveal what's known as the "Multitasking Bar." This bar shows the icons of all your open apps. That's right! Don't think that just because you hit the "Home" button to leave an app, that you've closed that app. Apps on any iOS device remain open until you actually close them. To view your open apps, you flick right or left. The most recently used app should appear first and, usually, they are in order from most recently used to longest ago used app from left to right, respectively.

Now, you may be saying, "Well, don't leave me hanging. If you don't close an app by going back to the home screen, how do you close it?" And, the answer would be, right from that Multitasking Bar. Tap and hold an icon until it wiggles, then tap the white minus sign in the red circle to the upper left of the icon of the app you wish to close. It's as simple as that! Now, to stop those icons from wiggling, just tap the Home button.

You can also access that Multitasking Bar by double clicking the Home button as I indicated earlier. Using that Multitasking Bar, it's possible to go from one open app to another if you need to work with multiple apps and, of course, that's where it gets its name from. If that's not fast enough access from app to app now that you've enabled multi touch gestures, you can swipe left or right, depending on which app you're in, with four or five fingers. As with the upward swipe to access the Multitasking Bar, you need to be sure you're using four or five fingers and not getting lazy with one of them during the swipe. Again, these gestures are all a matter of touch and sometimes take quite a bit of practice before your iPad will agree with you about exactly what you're doing and what it should do but, once you've got it, you'll be amazed at how efficient you'll be.

The final four or five finger gesture we'll discuss is the "Pinch." Ok you may be saying, "We did that already, goofy," but this is a little different. This you can do from within any app. Pinch using four or five fingers to reveal the home page. So, you see, there's another way to get to the home page. Once you've mastered it, and you will master it, you can use whichever method is easiest, most productive, and/or the most fun, or any of the above in any combination. Some of you may wonder why I'm using your reading time telling you to do the same thing in different ways, but believe me, others will find one or the other is their preference and will be glad they found out about the second way, so I hope you'll bear with me.

Wireless (or Wi-Fi) Syncing

In giving you an idea about some of the new features introduced in iOS 5.x and carried over to 6.x, I'd be remiss if I didn't mention Wi-Fi Syncing. As of iOS 5.0, technically you no longer need a computer. Updates can be done via an internet or Wi-Fi connection right from the device. The app store and iTunes are both available on the device itself so you no longer need access to iTunes on your Mac or PC to access additional content. Backups can be done to iCloud from the device, eliminating the need for backing up to your computer.

That being said, many baby boomers feel insecure about backing up all of their personal information to an unseen and unknown cyberspace storage device that they may not be able to trust. When I talk about trust, I am primarily referring to online security I'm not questioning Apple's integrity. Apple knows there will be people that cannot, or do not, trust such a service and have, therefore, built in a mechanism to bypass this if so desired. In iOS 5.x, through the time of this writing, at the very least (and I have no reason to believe, nor do I foresee, them changing this anytime soon) they have provided an option of Wi-Fi Syncing. Syncing (short for synchronizing) via Wi-Fi, occurs daily when your iPad is plugged into a power source, locked (the lock screen is showing), and on the same Wi-Fi network as your computer. This only happens if you've set it up to do so. In a subsequent chapter, I'll be showing you exactly how to do this. The bottom line is, your iPad and all content you decide you'd like on it, is transferred from iTunes (a free Apple App for your computer) to your iPad or any other iOS device you choose to set up that way. The existing set-up of your iPad, at the time of the sync, is stored on your computer, in iTunes, until the next sync. The whole process occurs seamlessly, without your knowledge, usually, under the above conditions - pretty awesome. Prior to this Wi-Fi syncing feature, it was necessary to physically plug your iPad into your computer each time you wanted to update the content of your iOS device. Now, after the initial set-up, you no longer have to make that physical connection between your computer and your iPad unless you choose to, you can do it, wirelessly, from any room that shares the network connection between both units.

I don't want to leave this chapter without giving another mention to iCloud. I've already mentioned that it is a file back up system that every owner of an iOS device or OSX 10.7.x, Lion operated, or better

Mac is entitled to access. To give you a little more information on the subject, account holders have access to 5Gb of free online storage that they can use to back up their units. Additional storage space is available for a charge should the need present itself, but 5Gb is generally plenty for most iPads, even the 64Gb models. I have a 64Gb model with over 350 apps as well as photos and other data and only use about 2.7Gb per backup. Currently, I'm using just over 4Gb but, to economize, will stop backing up email if the need arises. That is backed up on my computer already and there is no reason that would require me to back it up to iCloud, too, should I need the space for other things. But, as I say, I currently have over 33Gb of used space on my 64Gb unit. I only use a portion of my iCloud space even though my iPod Touch and iPhone are also backed up to that account (and I'm backing up everything on all devices).

Let me end this chapter by telling you about one of my other favorite features of iOS 5.x and later, and that is the Dictionary and Thesaurus that are built in. If you're unfamiliar with a word, highlight it by touching and holding it until a, what I can only describe as a magnified, appearance occurs. At that point let go and several options should appear. The options will vary based on the application you're in but, if you're in an editing or writing type app, you should have the option to "Select" or "Select All" among others. Choose "Select" and more options should pop up. In writing and editing apps both a dictionary and a thesaurus should be among them. It won't say that, it'll say "Define" and "Suggest." If you're looking for a thesaurus, choose "Suggest" and, naturally, if you're looking for the meaning of the word, choose "Define." When reading in many apps, the option to "Define" remains once a word is selected. To me, this is a wonderful feature that is shared with my Mountain Lion OSX MacBook Pro. I have used it many times and enjoy the ease with which I can get an answer to a quick question such as the use or meaning of a particular word.

Altogether, there were over 200 changes and/or new features introduced with iOS 5.x. There are far too many to review in detail in an overview in this chapter.

```
┌────────── CHAPTER 3 ──────────┐
│                               │
│                               │
│            iOS 6.x            │
│                               │
└───────────────────────────────┘
```

As with iOS 5.0, there are over 200 more features/updates introduced with this latest upgrade. Don't let that scare you. If you've been holding off on upgrading because you just got to know iOS 5.x, get a copy of this book, follow along, and dive right in.

Chapter 3, like Chapter 2, will be an overview of some of the new features, but an overview can't do justice to some of those changes. Those particular features will have dedicated chapters. One of the main features introduced to the iPad with iOS 6.0 was, of course, Siri on the iPad third generation and later. Unfortunately, the original iPad will not be able to update to iOS 6.0 and the iPad 2 will not have the ability at the time of release of iOS 6.1 at least, to utilize Siri. Siri, as many iPhone 4S and later owners know, is a fun and informational little addition to the newest iPad and, with iOS 6.0, its functionality was greatly enhanced. Prior to the release of iOS 6.0 which enabled the iPad third generation to utilize this feature, I saw little reason to upgrade from an iPad 2 to iPad 3. The primary changes were the Retina Display which was amazingly clear, the improved cameras, mainly the rear facing one, 4G, and the upgraded processor. None seemed to be earth shattering, and I didn't feel that they necessarily merited the higher price tag. An upgrade from iPad 1 to the third generation made a lot of sense to me at the time, if you could afford it. The introduction of Siri on the iPad, with iOS 6.0, changed that for me. I would now say that it may, very well, be worth the upgrade to a third generation model, again depending on your financial situation and your desire to try out new and different technologies.

Now for some of the features introduced with iOS 6.x. As I said, there's Siri for iPad third generation and above. That's a big difference. The iPad 3 offered dictation abilities prior to Siri, but Siri will also take notes, write email messages, open apps, and search the internet for things you have a question about. Not to mention the fact that she's just plain entertaining. I say that notwithstanding the fact that she can also be quite infuriating. When you're trying to express yourself to an AI (artificial intelligence) equipped device and that AI personality doesn't "Get it," you can get to the point of wanting to pull your hair out. OK, so that's me; that may not be you. I'll give you that, but you've got to admit she can sometimes be very frustrating. I don't know how many times while training her to my voice and inflections, she told me "I don't know but I can search on the internet for 'Go jump in the lake!'"

Another feature of iOS 6.x that I think many of you will like is called "Privacy" in settings. With the Privacy setting, you can control what apps have access to which data with much more control than with previous releases. Along the lines of Privacy, there's also "Do Not Disturb" in settings. When "Do Not Disturb" is enabled, a moon icon shows at the top of your iPad screen, next to the time. Messages won't ring through unless you've allowed their call on your favorite list (another new item), you've otherwise enabled their messages in Notification settings, or you've enabled "Repeated Calls" in Settings -> Notifications -> Repeated Calls. If that is enabled and you get a second call from the same person within three minutes of disconnecting, that message will ring through. If you choose to turn "Do Not Disturb" on, you can schedule it for the times you would like it to be effective. This feature can also be scheduled on an ongoing basis between set hours.

An app undergoing a huge transformation with the new operating system is the Maps app. Gone are Google maps. They've been completely replaced by Apple's own Maps. More on this will be forthcoming when we cover them in Chapter 11.

As in the introduction of iOS 5.0, there are far too many changes to list here. Hopefully, I'll do many of them justice when we get to the specific apps. For now, let's just say this new release is impressive.

CHAPTER 4

Keyboard Shortcuts

A pple has assisted users in every way possible so that they get full enjoyment and utility from these marvelous devices. Some of the nice touches that are incorporated into the operating system are the number of keyboards available. Not only are there keyboards for multiple languages, but there are keyboards that vary based on the app you happen to be in at the moment. An example of this would be, when you're in Safari and attempt to enter a character into the address bar (that's the browser's address bar, not the Google search box), a keyboard will pop up and that keyboard will have a ".com" key on it. If you tap and hold that key for a few seconds, you'll be presented with several other options, they are ".net", ".org", ".us" and ".edu". How much easier can they make that!

You'll notice that, when you're in email, the keyboard will have an "@" sign. If you're astute, you'll notice several, or sometimes many, modest changes to the keyboard that pops up in various apps. Along with these changes, there are a number of shortcuts that will assist you in your usual hunt and pecking, or mastery of the keyboard, whichever the case may be. I'll go over a few in this chapter and, as you become accustomed to your iPad, you may find even more.

First, something that is almost a necessity to know, to type all caps, you double tap the shift key. It should turn blue when activated. To inactivate it, tap it once again. Now to get this feature to work, it must be enabled in settings. Go to Settings -> General -> Keyboard -> Enable Cap Locks, and turn it on. This should be turned on by default, but it doesn't hurt to check it, especially if you're having difficulty activating the feature.

Sometimes you'll want to just type an apostrophe and be in a hurry. Rather than change the keyboard to the numeric keyboard by tapping the ".?123" key, tap and hold the exclamation mark on the top keyboard for a few seconds. The apostrophe should appear. In iOS 5.x you only needed to hold it for a few seconds and it would insert it; however, in iOS 6.0 and up you need to slide your finger onto it. Don't lift your finger until after you've slid it onto the apostrophe. Don't worry if you slide your finger up to it but change your mind about typing it. The selected keyboard character will not be inserted until you lift your finger. So, if you tap the exclamation mark, but decide what you really wanted to type was the letter "S", don't worry about it, just slide your finger across the keyboard, without lifting it, and go to the "S" key before lifting your finger up.

As with the apostrophe, quotation marks can be handled right from the regular keyboard by tapping and holding the "?" key. To type a dia-critical mark above or below a letter, tap and hold the letter in question and a variety of options will appear. Slide your finger to your selection and it will appear in your document.

If you need to type currency signs other than the USD sign, "$", go to the numeric keyboard and tap and hold the "$" sign. You will be presented with options for typing five other currency symbols, including Euros and British Pounds.

To type the section sign (§), tap and hold the ampersand (&) on the numeric keyboard. To type a bullet or your choice of hyphen lengths, tap and hold the hyphen sign on the numeric keyboard.

For word or phrase shortcuts, go to Settings -> General -> Keyboard -> Add New Shortcut. Enter your phrase and abbreviation and, whenever you type that letter combination, your phrase will appear. For that reason, I suggest you make your letter combination unique or unusual so that you don't end up entering your phrase every time you type a word with the set letter combination.

To give you an idea of how you can use this feature, I have common email closings as "Shortcuts." Love, Sheila - Love, Grandma - Love, Mom - Best Wishes, Sheila - etc. For letter abbreviations I wouldn't use "ls" because those letters appear together commonly. Instead, I use "l,s".

Now, as I say, this is not a comprehensive list, you'll probably find more as you experiment with and use your iPad more, but it's a good enough list to get you going with the more commonly used shortcuts.

Splitting the Keyboard

Some people, particularly men with bigger fingers, find it much easier to "Thumb" type on smartphones and tablets. This next feature eases that style of letter entry. Go to Settings -> General -> Keyboard and turn "Split" on. Then, when you want a split keyboard, press and hold the typewriter key. "Split and Undock" will appear as an option. Slide your finger up to select that option and the keyboard will move up to the center of the page and be split half on the right side of your screen and the other half on the left half. Now you can "Thumb" type all you want.

To re-dock the keyboard, tap and hold the typewriter key again, then slide your finger up to "Dock and Merge."

CHAPTER 5

Syncing Your iPad

Now that you're somewhat familiar with the basics of your iPad, the next step is to set it up for ongoing care. As I noted earlier in this book, you can pretty much be computer free, if you choose, once you've updated to iOS 5.0 or later. If you don't own a computer, you can bypass this section entirely. If you do own a computer, I suggest setting up some of the features to sync with that computer.

Try to use the computer you'll be syncing with in the future because, the way the "i" devices are currently set up, it's difficult, but not impossible, to change computers once you've set up your sync preferences and synced with one. Naturally, computers don't last forever and, at some point, you may need to replace your existing computer. As I say, it's possible to swap out computer syncing to do so with a different one, it's just not an easy process because you can only sync with one iTunes music library at a time. Also, if you're not backing up to iCloud, all of your backups are on the old computer and that data needs to be backed up on the new one when you switch over. I won't get too into detail about switching computers once you've synced. This book is intended more as a reference for initial and ongoing set up and iPad utilization. To switch computers once a previously synced system dies, you'll find information on the Apple.com website explaining the process.

The first step in your initial synchronization is to connect your iPad to your computer, be that a Mac or a PC, once you have the latest version of iTunes installed on it. As noted earlier, iTunes is a free app that is available from the Apple site. iTunes handles and stores your music library on your computer as well as movies, podcasts from the iTunes store, and a number of other media content items. iTunes itself has undergone a transformation at the same time as Apple's new mobile operating system was being released. Some features may look a little differently by the time you read this, as these things change like the wind but, once iTunes is updated/installed, on a Mac, go to iTunes -> Preferences -> Devices and, I suggest, check "Prevent iPhones, iPods, and iPads from Syncing Automatically." What this does is allows you to do whatever you want in iTunes, when your device is connected, without having things you want to change synced first. Once you make your desired changes, you can manually sync without a problem.

Next go to the "Store" tab in Preferences, and select those items you want iTunes on your computer to download when purchases are made on your device. In other words, if you purchase an app on your iPad and want it to be reflected in your iTunes app on your computer, check the "Apps" box, and so on. I select all three boxes, Books, Apps, and Music, because I always want my iTunes Library on my Mac to be identical to my iOS devices as far as maximum content goes. In this way, even if I don't install a particular app on my iPhone after installing it on my iPad, I always have an option to do so by checking that app for that device in iTunes. More on that in a minute and I think it will be cleared up. Also, while on that tab, check the box "Always Check for Available Downloads."

The last thing you can do in Preferences is go to the "Sharing" tab and turn on "Home Sharing" if you'd like. What this does is makes the media on your computer, available for playing via your device and vice versa. Again, this is an option of which you may not choose to avail yourself. If you're undecided, you can always do it at a later time. If you do decide to do it, it will also be necessary to turn it on on your device. On your iPad go to Settings -> Music -> Home Sharing and log in with your Apple ID. You are now all set to mix your content between devices and play it through a variety of speakers.

If you have a PC instead of a Mac, everything will be basically the same except you'll access these "Preferences" via "Edit" on iTunes toolbar then select "Settings." From there, just go to the aforementioned tabs and follow the directions provided above for "Preferences."

Your First Computer Sync

Now that your "Settings" or "Preferences" have been set up, connect your iPad with the USB cable provided with it. iTunes will recognize your "i" device and register it for you.

The serial number of your device will appear in the iTunes window and, if an update is available for the device, you will be informed and offered an opportunity to upgrade then and there, via iTunes. If your iPad firmware and software are up-to-date, the first time you connect you'll be asked to give your iPad a name. You can name your iPad anything you'd like in order to keep it recognizable and differentiate it from other iOS devices that may be synced with that same computer. Something simple is fine like "MyName" iPad or, if you have more than one iPad, "MyName" iPad 2, where "MyName" is replaced with your actual name.

Three Ways to Sync

There are now three ways to sync your iPad or other iOS device with your computer. We'll start with the old fashioned way - connecting to your computer physically. To sync with iTunes in this fashion, follow along with these instructions:

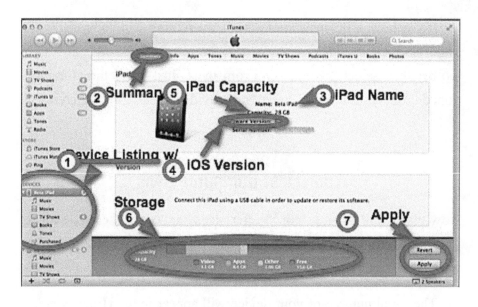

iTunes Sync With USB - Connect Your iPad to Your Computer

1) Select Your Device in the Left Column, Under Devices

2) Select the Summary Tab

3) Name Your Device

4) If Your iOS Version is Not the Latest, You Will Be Able to Update

5) You Can View Your iPad's Total Capacity

6) You Can View Your iPad's Total and Appropriated Capacities

7) This is the Apply Button You'll Use to Save Your Settings Once Finished With the Set Up Process

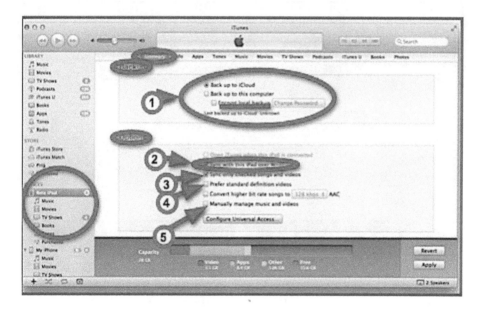

While Still In the Summary Section, With Your iPad Selected

1) Choose Whether to Back Up to iCloud Or Your Computer - Don't Choose Both, But Definitely Choose One or the Other

2) No Matter Which Way You'll Back Up, You Can Also Choose To Sync Over Wi-Fi or Via USB as You Are Now

3) You Can Choose to Have iTunes Only Sync Songs and Videos That You've Checked or Selected as Opposed to All

4) You Can Choose Here to Download Your Videos in a Standard or High Definition (HD) Format - See More on This Choice In This Chapter

5) You Can Set iTunes Up So That You'll Only Manually Manage Your Music and Video Downloads as Opposed to Letting iTunes Automate the Process

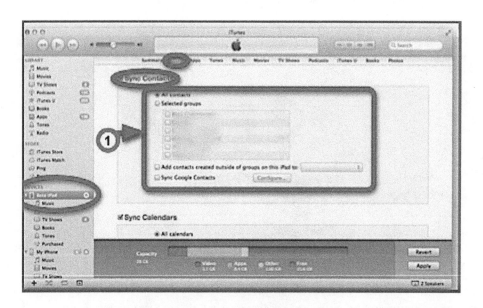

1) With Your iPad Still Selected, Move Over to the Info Tab

2) At the Top of the Page, Choose Whether or Not to Sync Your Contacts - See More on This In this Chapter

3) In Box Indicated By the Number 1, You Can Choose to Sync: All Your Contacts; Selected Groups of Contacts - If You Have Groups in Your Address Book; Contacts Created Outside of Groups on Your iPad to:; or, Sync Google Contacts

Scrolling Down the Info Page

1) Choose Whether or Not to Sync Calendars, Again You Can Select All Or Particular Ones

2) Choose the Amount of Time You Will Sync Events For

3) NOTE: You Are Informed That You May Have Duplicate Entries If You Both Back Up and Sync Your Contacts, Calendars, etc.- See More on This In This Chapter

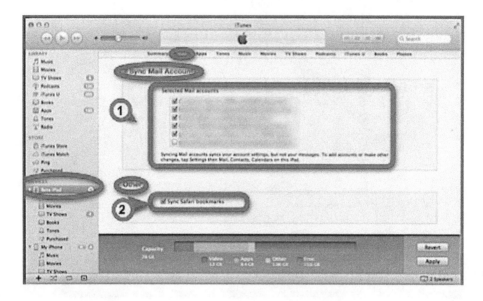

Remaining On the Info Page, Further Down You' ll Find

1) An Option to Sync All Mail Accounts Or Accounts of Your Choice

2) Under the "Other" Category You Can Choose to Sync Safari Bookmarks -

Note: Only Safari Bookmarks Will Sync, No Other Browsers

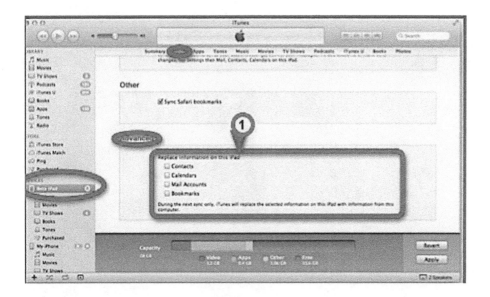

Finally, At the Bottom of the Info Page We Come to Advanced.

1) DON'T Do Anything Here Unless You Ever Get So Mucked Up on Your iPad That You Want To Pull Your Hair Out. Then, As a Last Resort, You Can Come Here and Set Your iPad Back to the State It Was In When You First Set It Up, With Only Those Things You Select On It.

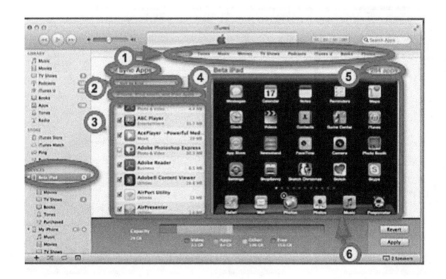

Moving Along the Tabs From Left to Right

2) Next Select the Apps Tab

3) You Can Sort Your App Listing by Several Factors

4) You Can Select Which Apps to Sync With Your iPad - NOTE: Each iOS Device Can Be Set Up Individually, Selecting the Apps You Want on Each By Selecting the Device Under Devices and Making Your Choices

5) You'll Notice That I Have Sorted My Apps By Kind So They Are Broken Down Into iPhone Apps, iPad Apps, And All Apps

6) On the Upper Right Of the Home Screen Image Is a Number Indicating How Many Apps Are Installed on This Device. You'll Notice I Only Have 284 Apps Installed On This iPad - On My 64Gb 4G Model I have Over 400

7) This Is An Image of Your Home Screen. Outside of This Picture Are the Subsequent Pages Pictured in a Column Down the Right Side

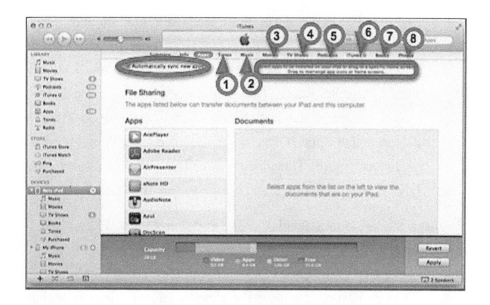

To Finish Up Working With Apps, You Can Select the Box If You Choose To Automatically Sync New Apps

1) Now Move Along the Top Tabs First Going to Tones

2) Music

3) Movies

4) TV Shows

5) Podcasts

6) iTunes U

7) Books

8) and, Photo. Continue to Make Selections in a Similar Fashion. When Through, Go Back to the Summary Screen and Make Sure You've Only Chosen One Back Up Method, Then Click "Apply" and Your iPad Will Sync. NOTE: The First Time You Do This,

I Highly Recommend You Sync Only to Your Computer to Get All Your Contacts, Calendars, etc. Onto Your iPad. When the Sync Is Completed a Few Minutes Later, Go In and Uncheck Those Sync Selections That Will Give You Duplicate Entries - i.e. Contacts, Calendars, Notes - and Choose to Back Up to iCloud at that Point If That Is Your Choice. I've Found It To Be a Cleaner Way of Transferring Your Data Without Messing Up Organizational Settings You May Have In Your Contacts, etc.

Just a few important details I'd like to point out that weren't necessarily covered in the above instructions. First, you can decide on the Summary page what the clarity of your High Definition Videos should be, i.e. 720p or 1080p. 1080p is the clearest High Definition setting, and available on the iPad 3rd generation and later, but the files are also much larger taking up more of your precious space on your device. The difference in the quality of the video may not be so much different that it merits larger storage. If, on the other hand, you really enjoy watching videos on your iPad and want them to be as clear as possible, you can always choose the 1080p option and remove the video from your device after viewing, or transfer it to a Wi Drive (more about this option in the chapter on Peripherals) or other comparable option, clearing space for other movies. To download Videos at the 720p or 1080p Hi-Def settings, you don't have to do anything. To save space and view in standard definition, check the box on the Summary page indicating this option.

I also want to point out that, should you choose to download in standard definition, the conversion process takes a little bit longer so your syncing will initially be slower. If you'll be doing your viewing from your iPad through your hi-def TV set, you may elect to retain the hi-def formatting. It will make a visible difference there.

Similarly, you can choose to convert your audio by checking the applicable box on the same page. Audiotechs maintain it makes a noticeable difference. To the average listener like me, we probably couldn't tell the difference.

If you set up Mail syncing between your computer and iPad, only the settings sync, not your actual mail. So don't worry that syncing your mail account will import all the mail from your computer into your mail account on your iPad, it doesn't. But, for ease of set up, all the settings will be synced over.

Also, if you choose to backup your iPad to your computer, you can encrypt those backups in the settings on this page. This option is not available via iCloud backup. The final point is, the Apply button I pointed out in the instructions does not always appear. At times, when no changes have been made to your settings, that button shows as Sync. They do basically the same thing, but Apply saves the changes you've made before it does the actual sync.

The second way of syncing your iPad is over Wi-Fi. We went over the selection for that in the aforementioned instructions. The only difference in set up is that you would select that option on the summary page. This was a new option introduced with iOS 5.0 and, I believe, one of the best features introduced with that version as far as convenience goes.

Wi-Fi syncing takes place automatically each time you plug your device into a power source and it is on the lock screen, the initial screen that comes up when you hit the home or power buttons. This eliminates the necessity for thinking about when or how you did your last sync, it just does it for you. I personally back up to iCloud and sync over wi-fi, but not all my contacts or other entries that can be duplicated. As I pointed out to you, I only did that the with the first sync. Now, I just back those up to iCloud.

The final method of syncing is manually syncing. Assuming your settings have been made as we went along, manually synchronizing is as easy as 1-2-3. This can be done whenever you just feel the need, as when you've added apps to your computer and want them to update to your iPad or vice versa. In iTunes on your computer, select your iPad under devices and, when the page opens, click on the Sync button in the lower right corner.

On your iPad, go to Settings -> General -> iTunes Sync. Tap the right arrow and tap "Sync Now." That's all there is to it. No matter how you've set it up in your computer iTunes app, those settings will be applied by these manual syncs as well.

Setting Up iCloud Backup

Once you've enabled iCloud back up on your computer via iTunes, it's time to complete the process by doing so on your iPad. Go to Settings -> iCloud and enter your iCloud log in information which you should have created when you first set up your iCloud account on your computer or your iPad. If you haven't yet done so, you can do it now.

To enable iCloud Syncing/Backup on your iPad, after entering your iCloud information, tap Storage & Backup from within the iCloud settings. Turn iCloud Backup "On." Back out by tapping on your iCloud account ID at the top left of that column and Settings -> iCloud - Tap and enable/disable iCloud sync from within Settings for the following apps/features:

1. Mail
2. Contacts
3. Calendars
4. Reminders

5. Safari Bookmarks
6. PhotoStream
7. Documents and Data
8. Notes
9. Find My iPad

These features/apps are not mutually exclusive. You can set one up independent of the others or set all up simultaneously with no ill effects. Most of these have been or will be explained in more detail in the following chapters on built in apps, but let me give a little bit of background to a few.

PhotoStream has undergone a pleasant change in iOS 6.x. Photos in PhotoStream can now be shared with individuals of your choice. PhotoStream itself is a bit of a mixed bag. What happens with this feature is, when enabled, all photos on your iOS devices sync or mingle and appear on every other iOS device you have on the stream, as well as your computer if it's enabled there. They remain on your device for up to 30 days then are removed. If they're on your computer, too, they'll remain there, but not on your iDevices. There is also a 1,000 photo cap. So in any 30 day period that you exceed 1,000 photos in your stream, those photos will also be deleted from your device. Another good thing about PhotoStream is that none of your photo storage counts against your 5Gb iCloud maximum. PhotoStream photos and iTunes purchases are all stored free on iCloud.

In the initial iOS 5.0 versions, photos in PhotoStream couldn't be deleted from your device; that would have to be done on your main computer. That changed in version 5.1.1 but then albums couldn't be deleted from your device. I'll explain more of what happens now when we get to Chapter 21 on the Photos app.

Another point worth mentioning is that Notes sync with your Outlook notes on your PC or your Mail notes on OS X 10.6 through 10.7.4. In

45

10.8, Mountain Lion, OS X has its own Notes app with which these notes sync. Another nice feature of the iPad/Mountain Lion Duo.

Finally, I'd like to speak briefly about Find My iPad. This is a feature that has been in the news lately for both good and bad. Personally, I've had good experiences with it and, if it's used properly, I believe it's an excellent addition to the iPad and what it has to offer.

At one point, after setting up a student's Find My iPad feature in her iCloud settings, I received a frantic call from her telling me that she had lost her iPad and didn't know what to do with herself. As I tried to calm her, I told her to go to her computer and enter iCloud.com into the address bar in her browser. She did so as I waited. Once there, I asked her to click on Find My iPhone. As she did so, the map honed in on her own address and showed her as being within feet of the iPad itself. She turned and saw it sitting in the same room on an opposite wall. Needless to say, she was greatly relieved.

Had it been a less happy ending where she found it missing on the other side of town, knowing that she hadn't taken it there, she could have sent a message to the other party, sounded an alarm, locked the screen, and/or remotely wiped the iPad clean. Had it later been recovered, she very easily could have restored it to its previous condition via her iCloud backup which I had also set up for her. The key here, I think, is acting as quickly and effectively as possible. Better to be safe than sorry. Had she simply found it missing nearby, the alarm she might have sounded could have alerted her to its exact location. There are many positive scenarios that can come out of this. Weigh these very well against whatever negatives you may hear in these regards before making your choices.

File Sharing

Getting Your Documents From Here To There

With the introduction of iCloud and other Cloud services, there are a number of ways to get files from your iPad to your computer and back again but, one of the most straight forward, remains via iTunes. For other methods, it's usually a matter of learning the features and nuances of a new app, such as Dropbox or Box.net.

For iTunes file sharing, though, just follow along with the following instructions:

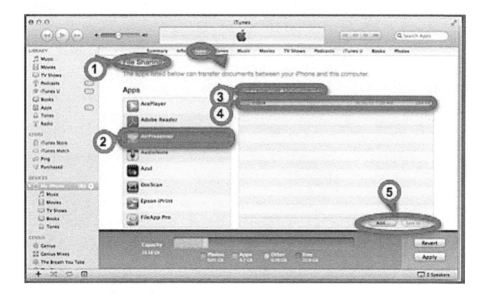

Under the Apps Tab, With Your iPad Still Selected

10) Scroll Down to File Sharing

11) Select the App that Has the Files You Want to Transfer From/To

12) You'll See the App Documents Listed, Filled In With the Apps That Currently Exist on Your iPad

13) Select the Documents You'd Like to Transfer

14) Depending On Whether You're Saving to Your Computer or Adding to Your iPad, Choose the Applicable Button

That's All There Is to File Sharing Via iTunes. Name Your Files and They Will Appear on Both Your iOS Device and Computer.

PART TWO
Built In Apps

CHAPTER 6

Settings Top to Bottom

Overview

In this Chapter, we'll discuss settings in general. That's not to say "General Settings." Some of the settings we'll review here will be covered in greater detail in chapters dealing with the specific app that they control.

Although Settings is said to be one of the iPad's built-in apps, I like to think of it more as a control box that regulates the behaviors of other apps. Generally, the settings for individual apps are self-explanatory but there is some shorthand involved and, as usual, there are technical settings that need explanation even if only to say, "You don't need to adjust that setting!"

Since iOS 6.0, settings have changed slightly from version 5.1.1 with some nice additions being included, especially in regards to privacy settings. In earlier versions, Apple was sometimes criticized for allowing apps to access more personal data than necessary for them to function properly. The apps were required to request access, for example, to photos but would then be able to download those photos unnecessarily and would then have those photos at their disposal without any further controls.

Being well known for their security precautions, this became quite an embarrassment for Apple and they immediately worked to close any loopholes that would allow this type of unfettered access in the future. Since iOS 6.0, those loopholes have been closed even tighter. Now, it's necessary for apps to request, very specifically, the features that they must have access to in order to perform their assigned tasks. Users can make decisions, and change those settings if they so desire, within settings on an app by app basis.

For security purposes, if an individual sees that an app is requesting access to their contacts to adjust screen brightness, for example, they should not grant that access. Users should use their discretion in allowing apps to access personal data if they suspect the data may be misused or abused by a particular app.

I would be remiss in not pointing out that, even the Settings icon on the home screen has changed slightly in iOS 6.0 and the cogs in the wheels now turn, albeit slowly but surely. That being said, we will begin to review iPad settings from top to bottom.

From the Beginning

Airplane Mode

The first setting users see when opening the settings app is "Airplane Mode." When enabled, or "On," it disables internet usage and the usage of any apps that require internet or Wi-Fi access to function. It also disables, or turns off, "Bluetooth" which means the use of wireless headsets, keyboards, and/or other peripherals that require bluetooth connections. Bluetooth is the technology that allows devices to communicate wirelessly for short distances (usually less than 30 feet) using short wave radio transmissions.

Airplane Mode would be turned on, of course, while on a flight. These days, many airlines offer their own on flight Wi-Fi access. Once the captain authorizes it, it is possible to re-enable bluetooth so you can watch and listen to your iPad videos, music, and such with your wireless headset so you do not disturb other passengers. You can also leave Airplane Mode enabled and turn Wi-Fi on to access the plane's own in flight Wi-Fi service. Accessing your own 3G or 4G wireless signals is still not allowed on flights, so you must leave Airplane Mode on or your iPad off.

Wi-Fi

The next setting in order is "Wi-Fi." Most of you probably have heard and are familiar with the term Wi-Fi these days so I won't go into great detail here. Wi-Fi, which stands for "Wireless Fidelity," deals with the use of high frequency signals that transmit data over distances of approximately 200 feet or less in local area networks (lans).

The Wi-Fi setting is a little more involved than Airplane Mode. If you tap "Wi-Fi" in settings, you'll see, at the top, an "On/Off" switch. When "On," you should be able to access any open networks within range. When enabled, or turned on, "Choose a Network..." should show before the next session with a "spinner" of sorts after it. Local area networks within range should be listed. If there is a lock after the name of a network, it means that it is a secured network and you need a password or key to access it.

At the bottom of the list of available networks will be "Other..." with an arrow after it. If the network you want to access is a hidden network, or otherwise not showing, you can select that option and fill in the necessary details to access it. You will need the network name, the type of security, and the password to access it. Once you have added that network, it should show in your list of available networks and you can select it in order to access it.

Networks that are already listed have an arrow in a little blue circle at the end of the block they're listed in. If you tap that arrow, you'll see more settings. In most cases, access to these settings is unnecessary. Settings are pre-configured for most networks that you'll access. If you need to know the device's IP (Internet Protocol) Address, you'll find it here. In addition, you'll also find the subnet mask, router IP address, DNS (Domain Name Server), search domains IP, and client ID. These options will change if you change from "DHCP," to "BootIP," or "Static" under the IP Address tabs.

Another section deals with HTTP Proxy which, again, in most cases the average person will not need. If you're in a situation where a proxy is required, usually a business situation, the network administrator should be able to help you with the necessary settings.

Finally, you'll see a box for the URL of the proxy server if one was necessary. This box will not even appear unless a proxy server option has been selected or the setting is on "Auto." And I have left to last the "Forget this Network" button. This can be used if, in some instances, you need to access one particular of several different networks and the "Wrong" one keeps activating. When this happens, you can select that network and go in and tap "Forget this Network." Be warned, when this is done, any previous information or data you entered regarding that network is also forgotten and will need to be re-entered manually. Only use this if you are experiencing problems accessing a network because another continually selects itself and you don't usually use the network that is self-selecting. Otherwise, leave this setting or tab to tech support or other experts that deal with your iPad issues.

When you are done checking out or, in some instances adjusting these additional settings, back out of them by going to the top of the column and selecting the left facing arrow that says "Wi-Fi" to save any settings you have made.

Bluetooth

The next setting in order is "Bluetooth." As described earlier, this setting deals with short wave signals that power wireless peripherals such as keyboards, headsets, etc. When this is enabled, or "On," it uses more battery power. So, when not in use, it's best to leave it off unless battery consumption is not an issue for you or if you use bluetooth frequently.

"Pairing," or connecting, various bluetooth devices differs slightly based on the device you're trying to access but, to put your iPad in pairing mode so that it is discoverable by other bluetooth devices, turn it on. Once on, you'll see a "Devices..." section open which will list any devices it finds or that you are already connected to, even if not currently paired. While the spinner next to "Devices..." is in motion, your iPad is "Discoverable" or in a position to be "Found" by other bluetooth enabled devices.

When another bluetooth device is also in pairing mode, or discoverable, your iPad will find it and it will be listed here under devices. To actually pair it, some devices require the input of a code, usually something simple like "1-2-3-4" or "0-0-0-0". Once the code is entered correctly, the pairing is successful and you'll see a message indicating this. Most devices only require one pairing. When they are turned off, or disconnected, they will show as "Not Connected" or "Not Paired" but will remain listed as long as the iPad bluetooth switch remains "On." Future connections just require turning both devices on and having them within the required range of each other, again, usually about 30 feet.

Do Not Disturb (New in iOS 6.0)

New in iOS 6.x is a "Do Not Disturb" feature. When this setting is enabled alerts and FaceTime calls will not come through during designated times except as determined by the user when configuring it. Configuring "Do Not Disturb" is done in the next setting, "Notifications." When "Do Not Disturb" is enabled, a moon icon will appear in the status bar at the top of your screen, next to the time.

Notifications

The first feature/app that can be regulated in notifications is "Do Not Disturb." What this feature does, you will see above but how it functions is configured here. You can set it up so that "Do Not Disturb" is scheduled on an ongoing basis for certain hours that you determine. You can also decide who, if anyone, calls and alerts will be allowed from during those pre-set hours. If you decide on favorites, you can select your favorites from within your contacts or address book. Any "Groups" you have delineated in your Contacts will be listed under the "Groups" heading in the "Allow Calls From" tab if the arrow to right of it is tapped. The options under "Allow Calls From" are: Everyone, No One, Favorites, and any selected groups form within your contacts.

You can enable "Repeated Calls" so that any calls that come in from the same person within three minutes will come through unfettered and not be silenced.

Next in Notifications, users can set the order that notifications are received in manually or by the scheduled time of the particular alert. The next sections shows which apps are contained in "Notifications Center" and would therefore show on your Lock Screen when they come in or on your notifications screen, should you drag down from the top of your screen to reveal your notifications.

The next section, "In Notification Center," contains a listing of all apps that are currently contained in your notification area when you drag down your notification screen. Apps can be rearranged within this section by tapping the "Edit" button in the upper right of the column and dragging the tab in question to a different location. This controls the order in which apps will appear on your notification screen if all else is equal. In other words, if the sort order conditions set are the same and there is a pending notification for more than one app.

Within each app or feature, you can enable or disable notification center appearance, determine how many alerts from that app will appear at any one time within your notifications, select the alert style i.e. None, Banners, or Alerts, and turn on or enable Badge App Icons (the white number in a blue circle that appears on top of an app icon on your home screen. This number indicates how many alerts, etc. are available.), Additionally, you can set the apps ringtone, and determine whether or not an alert will appear on your lock screen (the screen that appears when your iPad screen first turns on that you need to "Unlock" with the slider). Now that was a mouth-full!

As you'll see in each app notification setting, a banner will appear for a few seconds then go away. It will remain on your notification screen when you drag it down, whereas an alert will remain until you act upon it. And, if those little badges or circled numbers on your home screen icons annoy you, you can go into the particular app in notifications and turn them off. No need to be nagged unnecessarily.

The final grouping in notifications are a listing of the apps that can be, but are not currently, in your notification center listings.

Sounds

General is next in settings but is so large, I will dedicate a separate section to those settings a little later on in this chapter. After General, comes Sounds. Within "Sounds" are ringers and alerts volume as well as enabling or disabling the physical volume controls on the side of your iPad. Under the Sounds section you can set the tones for: Ringtone, Text Tone, New Mail, Sent Mail, Tweets, Facebook Posts, Calendar Alerts and Reminder Alerts. You can also lock sounds so that your settings are not accidentally changed and, finally, you can turn off keyboard clicks if they get on your nerves. Personally, I like to hear the keyboard clicking away as I toil with emails and such but it does annoy many. If you're one of these people, just go into sound settings and disable keyboard clicks.

Brightness and Wallpaper

In adjusting your screen brightness, you have to balance ease of viewing with, again, battery use. The brighter the screen, the more battery that is used. If battery consumption is an issue for you, this is one way you can easily conserve it. I prefer to use the auto-brightness setting. In my opinion, this is a comfortable viewing mode that does not overload the battery.

Under the brightness setting is the Wallpaper section. You can choose a home screen and a lock screen wallpaper. They can be the same or different and they can be from your personal camera roll or from a preset photo included with your iPad. Just tap the right facing arrow to the right of the photo of your iPad and the various options will appear.

There are also apps, such as "Screen Oven," which are free and supply a number of other options that can be created, or are pre-made, within the app. I hold no stock in Screen Oven, and this is not a recommendation of it, just a mention of it as a free and available app that I have used and enjoyed. It has limitations and, I'm sure there are more and better apps out there, this is just an example of one of many that are available for screen savers and wallpapers for your iOS device.

Picture Frame

Picture Frame is a feature that can go pretty much unnoticed unless curiosity gets the better of you. While on your iPad lock screen, again, the opening screen with the slider, you'll see a little icon to the right of the slider with the image of a flower on it. If you tap that icon, you'll access "Picture Frame."

What Picture Frame is, is a slide show, of sorts, of photos that you have on your iPad. Which pictures appear in that slide show and how that slide show performs are determined here in picture frame settings in the settings app. The first section is for transitions. If you're not familiar with slide show or video transitions, they are segues from one photo frame to another. This setting determines what type of segue or action will occur between your various photos.

Dissolve is more or less self-explanatory. The image that is visible dissolves, or falls apart in little pieces, into the next image. Origami, on the other hand, if you've never seen, is very hard to describe. Similar to the process that it is named for, the Japanese art of paper folding, images "fold" and "unfold" into each other in various fashion. Origami is one of my favorite slide show transitions. If you've never experienced it, I highly recommend you give it a try if only to see what I'm talking about. I can assure you, I'm not doing it justice and don't pretend to be an expert on the art or the process. I've always thought of it as quite complex and have oversimplified it for the sake of ease of explanation.

After you decide which transition to use, and there are only the two to decide between, users set the amount of time each slide will appear. Options are: 2 seconds, 3 seconds, 5 seconds, 10 seconds, and

20 seconds. You can then decide whether or not to zoom in on faces, and if you'd like the app to "Shuffle," or mix the order of, your photos.

Finally, decide whether you'd like all photos on your device to be shown, or just particular albums on your camera roll.

Privacy (New)

Another new setting in iOS 6.x is "Privacy." As I pointed out earlier, Apple has attempted to tighten security measures around software creators' need for information to enhance functionality of their apps, and iPad owners' rights to control the use of their private information in all ways possible. Of course, if an application requires certain information to function properly and the user does not wish to allow the use of that information, their options are to curtail the ability of the particular app to live up to its potential, to uninstall the app all together, or to allow the requested access.

Within the Privacy setting are categories for Location Services, Contacts, Calendars, Reminders, Photos, and Bluetooth Sharing followed in the lower section by Twitter and Facebook. Each category has a right facing arrow to the right of the title which, when tapped, opens each category up to additional settings/permissions.

New in iOS 5.0, in iOS 6.0 the location services setting was removed from its own setting category and included in Privacy settings. Within Location Services, the first tab in "Privacy," users are able to enable or disable it completely. Location Services is another feature that places a large drain on battery power so, again, if that's a problem for you, you may wish to curtail the use of some of these options. What location services does, when enabled, is allow further enabled apps to access the user's exact location in its functionality. What this means, in essence, is that the user will be pinpointed on a map and their location will be communicated to the applicable program to enable it to reach peak performance. Although Apple is very good at screening apps that are included in the App Store and iTunes market, only the user can truly determine whether the function they want or need to be fulfilled is worth the level of privacy that they must relinquish to benefit from an app.

There are apps, such as the camera app, that need to have location services enabled if you want to benefit from their geotagging features. These features place you in a particular location, on a particular date and time, for future reference. In the example of the camera app, the place, date, and time the photo was taken will be included in its exif information so you can maintain a record of where you were during your two week vacation to the Bahamas in March 2012. EXIF stands for Exchangeable Image File Format, a standard for storing interchange information in image files, especially those using JPEG compression. Most digital cameras now use the EXIF format. There are other apps, as pointed out earlier, that don't really need access to your contacts to reach peak performance. In those instances, you should use your discretion to determine whether or not to grant access.

It is possible to enable location services overall then determine actual usage on an app by app basis. This is probably the best utilization of the location services feature. It allows you to utilize the best features of location services and leave the questionable ones out. Before moving on to the next section in location services, I'd be remiss if I didn't point out to you that, in my earlier example of the geotagging services feature with the camera app, you should keep in mind that any posting of those photos to social web sites like Facebook may also indicate where the picture was taken, and when in most cases. So, if you don't want that type of information included, use caution when taking and/or uploading those images to such sites.

The next section in the location services area lists installed apps that request location services information in their use. The camera app will be listed there, along with Siri, Maps, Find My iPad, and any other installed apps on your particular device that indicate such a necessity. Each of these can be enabled or disabled irrespective of the others. I highly recommend enabling this feature for Find My iPad. This "app" or feature is a marvel to behold.

Under this section, you will find legends explaining the symbols that may be shown next to applicable apps in the above listing. At the end of the legends will be an explanation of a "Geofence." This entire column on Location Services is much more informative than in the past. The reason for this is that Apple came under fire in the past for "Tagging" iPhone locations and using them to enhance their database of "Crowd-Sourced Wi-Fi Hotspot Locations." In theory, this database is updated, in an ongoing basis, by obtaining "Fixes" on iPhone and other iOS users' locations based on GPS and something known as triangulation. Triangulation obtains locations, in a very basic sense, by "bouncing" signals off of multiple cell towers and reading the response time back to the originating iOS device. Usually the number of towers used is three, thus the term triangulation. Of course, the process is much more complex than this but Apple uses a combination of this "Triangulation" and GPS positioning to set up and maintain their data base. This data base is then used to determine each iOS user's location. The information gathered by Apple does not personally identify iOS users or gather any information other than basic location from their devices according to Apple.

Now that I've totally confused you and opened myself up to all kinds of scientific and mathematics criticism, I'll go on with the final section in the Location Services tab, System Services. If you tap the arrow to the right of "System Services," you'll see that you can enable or disable, turn on or off, Compass Calibration, Diagnostics & Usage, Location-Based iAds, Setting Time Zone, and Wi-Fi Networking. And, at the very bottom of the column, the Status Bar Icon can also be enabled/disabled. The same legends apply to this section and, as I write this, a gray location services icon is located on the "Setting Time Zone" tab indicating that my location has been used within the last 24 hours for the time zone setting feature to work properly.

A quick look at these services will indicate that, in most cases, users can disable Location Services -> System Services -> Diagnostics & Usage, Location-Based iAds, and, in some cases, Setting Time Zone. Diagnostics & Usage is pretty self-explanatory but, you may be wondering what the heck Location-Based iAds means. For those of you who are curious it refers to Location-Based, Interest-Based Ads. Disabling this feature doesn't assure you of getting less ads from Apple, they just won't be specific to your location. To disable Interest-Based Ads all together, go to Safari on your iPad and enter **"Error! Hyperlink reference not valid.** in the address bar. You'll receive a "You have successfully opted out" message. You can always change your mind and reverse your action by going back to the same address in Safari and you will have opted in again.

Disabling the above services aids in retaining battery life and helps keep your iOS device as speedy as possible. If you back out of "System

Services" by tapping the "Location Services" arrow in the upper left corner of the column, you will return to the apps, tapping "Privacy" will now return you to the other categories in the Privacy tab. These other categories are not nearly as detailed as Location Services and merely contain lists of all installed apps that have requested access to the particular category on your iOS device. The last one, "Photos," also provides you with a warning similar to the one I've previously given you about the possibility of photos containing more personal information in their EXIF tags.

General

The remainder of the settings will either be covered in detail when we review the specific app involved or, as in the case of the lower left column apps listing, you'll have to decide on an app by app basis what settings you choose to employ for a particular program. This takes us back to the "General" settings category. General settings, like Location Services, encompass a wide range of features and we'll review them here.

One of the first settings you'll probably find yourself using is the Settings -> General -> About setting. You can acquire a significant amount of information about your device and its status from this setting alone. Here you'll get the low-down on your iPad and its various capacities. This is where you go to see what iOS version you're running. The About category tells you the number of songs, videos, photos, and applications you have on your iPad. It also tells you the capacity of your iPad or how much storage you have total and available. Finally, it details the version, model, serial number, Wi-Fi address, and bluetooth information for your iPad.

At the bottom of the page, you'll find diagnostics and usage info, legal notices (in very small print), license info, and regulatory info. One setting in there that you may want to be cognizant of is diagnostics and usage. If you tap the arrow to the right of that tab, you'll find that you may be automatically sending information about your iPad to Apple. If you are, you may decide to check "Don't Send" to again retain your privacy. The type of information that would be sent is not supposed to be personally identifiable, but I don't believe in automatically sending any information from my devices. I like to decide on a case-by-case basis.

One last thing you'll find in "About" is the name of your iPad. Here you can change the name of your iPad if you'd like. If you hate its name or have since acquired another necessitating a change, give it a try!

Software Update

This is where any new iOS updates will reside. If updates are necessary and your iPad is at version 5.0 or later, future updates can be completed right from your iPad. It's wise to check here in settings on occasion to see if updates are available since many updates address security issues or vulnerabilities.

Usage

Similar to diagnostics and usage, here you get a summary of usage statistics. You'll see how much space is used, available, and taken by various large apps. If you go into the apps listed, by tapping the right facing arrow, you'll see the actual size of the app and the amount of data within the app. You'll also find an iCloud summary in here. Detailed will be total storage, available storage, and an opportunity to manage storage by going into the documents and data totals. You can actually drill down and pinpoint exactly what files are taking up the most space within those large apps by tapping the arrows.

Finally, in usage, you'll be able to enable your iPad to indicate the percentage of battery life remaining at any point in time as well as view the amount of use and standby time since the last full charge.

Siri (New in iOS 6.0 and only relevant to iPad third generation or later)

Tapping the right facing arrow on the Siri tab will bring you to the controls for Siri itself. You can enable or disable it entirely within this tab. You also set the language and dialect, when voice feedback will be used, and designate your personal info from your contacts list. That's right, be sure that you yourself are listed in your contacts app to enable Siri to address you by name and refer to your email address, phone number, and street address when necessary. To utilize Siri, tap and hold the home button for a few seconds then speak. You need not hold the button while you speak, she will be activated by the initial tap.

VPN

This is simply where you enable or disable VPNs (Virtual Private Networks). These are mostly used with employers' networks to address firewall issues. Since anyone that needs that information will be able to get it from their network administrator, I won't get into detail about how that works or how to configure it here.

iTunes Wi-Fi Sync

This is where you go to force a "sync" with your computer. You can do this whenever connected to your computer or at anytime, as long as you're on the same Wi-Fi network, if Wi-Fi sync is selected in your device's iTunes settings on your computer.

Spotlight Search

This is where you enable the apps you want to include in searches that are done on your iPad. Searches are done fairly quick so enabling most, if not everything, is a good idea. Spotlight searches are done by flicking to the right while on the home screen. The home screen, for those of you who may have forgotten, is the screen you'll be taken to by tapping the home button (the button at the bottom, center of your iPad).

Auto-Lock

You might want to adjust this setting while reading this book to keep your lock screen from coming up too quickly while you're trying out these moves/adjustments. Options include: 2 Minutes, 5 Minutes, 10 Minutes, 15 Minutes, and Never. NOTE: The longer your screen remains lit, the more battery you use, so weigh what you're trying to do against how often it has to be done and try to strike a balance that will allow as much for both as possible.

Passcode Lock

If you want to password protect your iPad for security reasons, come here to the Passcode Lock setting and set it to "Turn Passcode On." You'll be prompted to enter a 4 digit passcode. To use a longer, more complex code, turn "Simple Passcode" Off. You'll be prompted to enter your existing passcode, then you'll be able to enter a more complex one if you choose. You'll have to input the new one twice before the setting is accepted.

You can also change your passcode here in this tab as well as decide when to require the passcode; i.e. Immediately, after 1 minute, after 5 minutes, after 15 minutes, after 1 hour, or after 4 hours.

Other options in this column include allowing Siri and Picture Frame access to your iPad when it is in locked mode. Finally, there is a setting that, if enabled, would erase all data on the iPad after 10 failed passcode attempts. Now that's security! If you choose to avail yourself of this option, don't worry too much as long as you've been backing up to either your computer or iCloud. You can always do a restore and put your iPad back into the same condition it was in prior to the erase action.

iPad Cover Lock/Unlock

This is where you enable Apple's Smart Cover (and other comparable covers) to lock and unlock your screen when they're opened or closed.

Note, this will not appear unless you have a smart cover or other cover capable of locking and unlocking the screen. The iPad is pretty smart, isn't it?

Restrictions

If you'd like to set parental/managerial restrictions on your iPad for any reason, this is the setting you'd look for. You can enable controls that would prohibit specified usage of your device under set conditions, but first you'll be prompted for a restrictions passcode. You can restrict individually listed apps, Siri, and explicit language.

Additionally, you can allow or restrict all content, or content based on ratings in a particular country. In the categories of music and pod-casts, movies, TV shows, books, apps, and you can also restrict in-app purchases. Each of these categories can be set independent of each other. You then determine when you want a passcode to be required; Immediately or after 15 minutes.

The next section in restrictions deals with privacy. This section is basically a reiteration of the Privacy category settings that we've previously discussed. Following the privacy section are those elements you decide to allow changes to, specifically accounts - mail, contacts, calendars, and volume limit.

In the final section users can enable restrictions for multiplayer games and adding friends in game center.

Use Side Switch To

You'll recall the switch on the side of your iPad that we discussed in Chapter 1 that controls muting your device. This setting can change the function of that switch to that of a screen rotation lock instead if you'd like. If, while working on your iPad, the screen keeps flipping from landscape mode to portrait mode and vice versa and is driving you absolutely crazy, you can slide the switch down. When lock screen is enabled, your screen will be locked in whichever mode it was in when you "Locked" it. To unlock it, slide the switch back up.

Note, you can't have it both ways. You can only use this switch as one or the other at a time, not both. So, in other words, once set as a lock screen switch, it will not function as a mute switch at the same time. The reverse is also true. However, you can come to this setting and change it back and forth at any time you wish.

There is another way to lock rotation if playing around with this adjustment doesn't suit your fancy or if, for any reason, it is not convenient at a given moment. We discussed the Multitasking Bar a little in Chapter 1. If you're accessing the Multitasking Bar, flick your fingers to the right sliding the bar to the left. All the way to the left of that bar will be a little semi-circle image. Tapping that image also locks your screen rotation in whichever mode you are in at the time. To unlock, just tap again.

MultiTasking Gestures

We discussed this setting in Chapter 2, *iOS Features* when we covered multitasking so I don't have much more to say here except to point it out to you again. If you want to enjoy this convenient, if not temperamental, feature, you'll need to come to this setting and activate or enable it. Just a reminder, this setting deals with four and five finger gestures on your iPad screen.

Date & Time

This is simply where you set either a 24-hour time setting, better known as military time, or a standard clock function. You can also set up your time zone and set the clock to keep time automatically.

Keyboard

The first section deals with: Auto-Capitalization, Auto-Correction, Check Spelling, Enable Caps Lock, and the "." Shortcut - which simply means that double tapping the space bar will insert a period followed by a space. Turning any of these features "On" will enable them so that they will perform their stated functions.

The second section deals with two settings. The first of which allows you to select various keyboards, primarily international. I say primarily because this is where you can also set the emoticons feature. Emoticons, for those of you unfamiliar with the term, are the "Smiley Face" variations that you see in email, text messages, and instant messages, to name a few. That's right, you can enable the "Emoji" keyboard here which will provide you with a number of options for your smileys. Since iOS 6.0, the number of available faces has increased even more over previous iOS releases.

To enable a keyboard, tap the right facing arrow to the right of the word "Keyboards" and select "Add New Keyboard." A number of international keyboards are available, Emoji among them. Once selected, if English was one of your choices, you can drill down further by tapping the named tab and choose the type of keyboard; i.e., Qwerty, Azerty, Qwertz as well as the hardware keyboard layout. This applies to some other keyboards as well, again depending on the language selected. Don't worry if you accidentally select the wrong international keyboard. Just go to "Edit" in the upper right corner of the column and tap the little white dash in the red circle next to the wrong keyboard, or the one you don't want to select, and tap "Delete." When finished selecting and setting up your desired keyboards, tap "Keyboard" on the upper left side of the column to go back to your other keyboard options.

Next comes "Split Keyboard" which we covered when we discussed keyboard shortcuts in Chapter 4. I will only point out, again, that this is where those adjustments are made.

The final section in the keyboard tab is for shortcuts. This is one of my favorite time savers on the iPad. If you have a phrase you use often, even an email closing, you can "Add New Shortcut," enter the phrase, and then assign a shortcut for it. In the future, when you type the shortcut combination, your phrase will appear in its place. Try to assign shortcuts that are not commonly found together in words such as letter combinations that would combine to form words or partial words. Characters, such as a /, -,!, and ? are fine in combination with other letters. If you go against my advice and use letter combination shortcuts that are frequently used in everyday language, you may find that your phrase appears all over the place in your writing! Don't say I didn't warn you!

International

This section mirrors the keyboard section we just discussed but adds settings for regional formatting and calendar type settings. The calendar types available are; Gregorian, Japanese, and Buddhist. I just want to point out that, once your decisions are made, they will appear on the right side of the applicable tabs so you can verify you have chosen the option you want. In the case of "Keyboards," the number of keyboards chosen will appear.

Accessibility

Here you'll find all the settings to assist visually handicapped, hard of hearing, and mobility challenged individuals. Apple has done a good job of incorporating features to address the needs of the disabled. If or when any of you need these settings, they are fairly self explanatory and the best thing to do is basically to play around with them and tweak them until you're comfortable with using your iPad and the various accessibility functions you've set up. See Chapter 1, *Getting to Know Your iPad* for more specifics.

Profile

This only appears if you've set up separate identifiable devices, such as an eye-fi which we'll discuss a little bit in another chapter.

Reset

This setting speaks for itself. If all else fails you can always come here and reset your device. There are several options here but it's best to stay away from it, unless you absolutely need it, so that you don't accidentally hit the wrong thing. Just know that these options are available if you're in a fix. We'll discuss some of these options in more detail when we get to *What to Do If Your iPad Gets Quirky.*

CHAPTER 7

Contacts

Overview and Set Up

G iven the fact that the Contacts app impacts, in one way or another, the functions of virtually every other built-in app in iOS, we'll begin our review of these built-in apps with an overview of it. Its effects are realized with all other apps that allow for messaging of any sort and include even apps that, on first thought, might not appear to be impacted by it at all, such as Safari, in which the completion of some forms are even based on your personal contact information. One might argue, since iOS 6.0 more than ever, the Contacts app is critical to the functioning of the iPad as a whole. Although the Contacts app itself has not seen many, if any, real changes in iOS 6.x, the way all other apps integrate with it are making the main difference in this iteration of iOS.

Since iOS 6.0, Facebook and Twitter integration are an integral part of most other apps, whether built-in or third party, and their ability to perform. Of course, this may be an overstatement when considering that some people don't use their iPads as communication devices in any sense of the word,. I still believe the mere potential of this app to have such a dominant role in iOS devices make it crucial to understand the function and operation of it.

That being said, when it comes down to actually using this app, it may be one of the most straightforward and relatively easy to grasp of all. The most complex part of utilizing this app, in my experience with students, is actually importing the majority of your computer or smartphone contacts to it. Due to this, you'll find most of the detailed instructions necessary in its use are in Chapter 5 on syncing your iPad. Here, we'll get into the actual mechanics of adding, editing, deleting, and finding individual/specific contacts.

Setting Up

As will be the case with many apps, the first step in using it is setting it up. Once the majority of your contacts have been imported, you're ready to begin using it. Go to Settings -> Mail, Contacts, Calendar -> Contacts and make your decisions as to your preference in viewing your contact information. Options are last name first, first name last or vice versa. Not too difficult, I think you'll agree. If that's the most difficult decision you have to make today, the rest of the day should be a cake walk. On the other hand, if you are agonizing over it, don't get too nervous, you can always change this later with no major repercussions should you find you don't like your first decision.

Besides setting your display preferences here, you can also set your sorting preferences in the same manner. Do you want your contacts arranged in alphabetical order by last name or by first, click on the right facing arrow to the right of "Sort Order" and make your selection. Again, this can always be changed at a later time or date.

Finally, but probably most importantly, you will select the contact information that you want used by various apps. To do so, you will need to have contact information entered for yourself, if this is the information by which you want to be identified.

Viewing Your Address Book

After opening your Contacts app, you will be faced with, what looks like, a regular, old-fashioned, address book. You'll see a listing of your contacts on the left, in alphabetical order. On the right will be the page containing the information for the first contact in the list or, if you've selected another one, whichever contact on the left is in blue text. At the top of the left page will be a red "bookmark" which says "Groups." Just below that will be a search bar which is then followed by the listing. On the extreme left edge of the left page, if you are in contacts as opposed to groups, is an alphabetical tabbing of each letter so that you can go directly to a tab when looking for a particular contact. Of course, you can also enter that first letter in the "Search" bar at the top to be taken to that category, so you have two options. The easier is probably entering the letter at the top since the tabs are pretty small even for tiny hands.

If you have your contacts broken down into groups, which we'll discuss later in this chapter, you can go directly to those groups by tapping the red bookmark at the top of the left page. Once you are in your group listings, you will see them broken down into two or three categories on the left page and the page on the right will have the red bookmark which will now say "Done." If you want to go to one of those group listings, select the group you're interested in and tap the "Done" button. You will then be taken to a page listing the contacts within that group.

Since iOS 6.0, besides an iCloud category, there is also a "Facebook" category, if you have set up Facebook in settings. Under the iCloud category, you will also find a breakdown of each of your other groups that are being backed up to iCloud. The only other thing to note is that, the listing of contacts is scrollable, so you can flick through it to view all of your contacts.

That wraps up the intro to the Contact app. Now for using it, read on!

Adding a Single Contact

Assuming you have imported the majority of your contacts by one of the methods detailed in the chapter entitled, *Syncing Your iPad,* there will likely be instances in which you will want to add to your contact list. Adding individual entries on an iPad is fairly intuitive in iOS 6.x if you have any experience with an address book.

First, go to the Contacts app and a page will come up, usually the last page you were on. In cases of the first use, the beginning of the alphabet will appear with your groups (if you have any) listed on the left of the "book." There will be a red page marker that will say "Groups" if you are in the contact list on a page other than your group listing (if you have any). When on the group listing page, it will say "Done."

If you want to see your groups, tap the red marker and you'll be taken there, (if you weren't already there). Tapping the marker when it says "Done" will take you to the last contact you viewed or your first contact listed alphabetically.

When viewing your contacts you'll see, on the left, a full alphabetical listing, based on your sort order, of your contacts. On the right will be an individual contact's information, depending on which you have selected on the left. When a contact in the list on the left is selected, their name turns blue. The contact information page will be scrollable if you have enough information on it to make it so. At the bottom of the contact information page are two buttons: "Send Message" and "Share Contact," which we'll discuss in a minute. Under those two options, there will be a third button and that will say "Edit" which, again, we'll discuss in a separate section.

If you examine the "All Contacts" page on the left, above the alphabetical listing of your contacts will be a search box and, on the bottom right-hand side of the page, a plus sign. To add an individual contact, you'll simply tap the plus (+) sign. A new page will come up with the cursor in the first name field. At the top of this new page will be the word "Info." To the left of that will be a "Cancel" button and, to the right, a "Done" button.

Eying the page further, you will see an "add photo" field along with the standard information fields that you would find on most address books. If you scroll down, there will also be a "notes" field and an "add field" section. Tapping the "add field" at the bottom will bring up a number of options for additional fields, one of which is "Birthday" and another of which is "Instant Message." Selecting and filling either of these fields will affect two other apps on your iPad, as will the "Twitter" field. The "Birthday" field affects the Calendar app, "Instant Message" affects your Message app, and, of course, the "Twitter" field affects any Twitter apps. Choosing any of the other options will only really affect the specific contact information presentation.

To enter your contact's information, go from field to field, filling out as many, or as few, of the fields as you desire. You'll note that the "Phone" field indicates "mobile;" however, if you want to enter a work, home, fax, or any other type of number, simply tap the "mobile" box and a drop down will appear with several other options in it. The listing should include most types of numbers you would ever want to deal with but, in the eventuality that your type of number is not delineated, there is an "Add Custom Label" option as well as an "other" option at the bottom of the list. If other doesn't cover it either, tap the "Add Custom Label" option and enter whatever you want to say to describe your phone number.

Next is the "Email" field. Again, selecting the "home" button will provide a drop down with additional options including a custom field choice. Once you've gone down the page and entered your information, you can also assign a "ringtone" if you've got a third party phone app, or a "text tone" by selecting one of the many options available in those drop downs. Should you choose to associate a photo of the contact with that contact's information, tap the "add photo" button. Two options will appear, "Take Photo" and "Choose Photo." Choosing photo will take you to your camera roll or photo stream images, and taking photo will take you to your Camera app.

When you're all done, tap the "Done" button on the top if you're satisfied with all your entries or, if you've totally changed your mind about adding this contact, the "Cancel" button on the top left. You'll be taken back to the contacts list and the contact information for the contact you just entered, if you selected "Done" or the last contact you selected, if you chose "Cancel." That's basically it for adding individual contacts. Relatively painless, I think, although you may disagree.

Editing or Deleting Contacts

How to Edit or Delete a Contact

Editing a contact is also fairly straightforward. To do so, go to the contact's information and tap the "Edit" button on the lower left side of the individual's page. The page will slide to the center of the screen almost entirely blurring the left page out of view.

At the top of the page, instead of showing the contact's name, will be a "Cancel" button on the top left, a "Done" button on the top right, and the word "Info" in the top center position. Under that will be the contact's name, company, and photo or add photo square, if no photo has yet been added. This will be followed by their phone number information, email, etc.

To make changes, just tap the line that you'd like to edit. As with a Mac, you must tap to the right of the information to delete any information that is already in the field since the only way to delete an entry is to backspace through it. There is no actual "delete" key like there is on a PC that will delete information to the right of the cursor, you must always backspace to delete.

Change any of the fields you would like to in this manner, scrolling through to the bottom of the page if necessary. To fully eliminate an entry, such as a phone number, you can tap the little white minus (-) sign in a red circle to the left of the phone number which will bring up a red delete key to the right of that entry. To complete the deletion tap the delete key and confirm. As with other deletions in other apps, if you've changed your mind, you can just tap "Cancel" to skip the delete action. If you realize you no longer wish to delete before you tap the red delete button, you can tap the little white minus (-) sign in the red circle again and the "Delete" button will disappear.

As you scroll down the page, you will see other "Minus" (-) signs in red circles as well as "Plus" (+) signs in green circles. Use these to add content such as another address or a new field. Finally, at the bottom, should you give up all hope of repairing the damage done to your entry, you can choose to delete the contact entirely. Of course, you may also choose to delete a contact just because they are no longer someone you need or want to keep track of, but keep in mind that you always have the option of erasing the contact entirely and starting from scratch, as may be the case if your best friend gets married, changes her name, moves to another state, gets a new phone number, and no longer wants a dog for her birthday (that would go in the notes section in case you think I've entirely lost my mind).

When you're done editing your contact's information, tap the "Done" button on the top right of the page or the "Cancel" button on the top left if you've changed your mind about completing your edits. When that's done, your page will "magically" slide back to the right of the screen and the left page will come back into full view.

Grouping Your Contacts

There may be occasions where you would like to categorize, or group, your contacts. An example would be a bridge club that you are a member of and whose members you would want to reach all together. If you sync over your contacts from your Mac this is easy to set up. You can create your groups in your Contacts, on Mountain Lion, or Address Book, on pre-Mountain Lion releases, and sync them over, which we covered in Chapter 5, *Syncing Your iPad*. From there you can add, edit, or delete additional contacts as previously described.

But not everyone has a Mac and there are other ways in which to add groups to your iPad. If you have a Windows PC, of course, there are third party apps such as CopyTrans - Contacts, which enable you to easily do this. However, another free option is iCloud.com. You can go to iCloud.com, sign in, select "Contacts" then follow these steps:

1. Select the red, bookmark, groups tab on the top of the page. It's the one with multiple people icons on it.

2. Click on the plus (+) sign on the bottom of the "Groups" page to add a group.

3. Enter the title or name of the group. Note: this can be changed later by clicking on it, deleting it, and entering a new one.

4. Now, click on "All Contacts" at the top of the column and all of your contacts should be listed on the right side.

5. Drag your contacts from the right into the applicable groups. A contact can go into more than one group and multiple contacts can be dragged at the same time by control clicking (on a PC), or command clicking (on a Mac) to highlight several then continue

holding the applicable key while you drag them to your desired group.

6. If you want to enter a contact into the group who is not currently in your contacts, just click the little plus sign on the right page and enter the new contact information. Once this is done, drag that new contact over as instructed above.

That's all there is to groups. Whether doing so on your Mac or in iCloud, as long as you backup to iCloud, the changes will be instantaneous. If you use a third party app you will, in all likelihood, depending on the app, have to sync upon completion. In addition to CopyTrans - Contacts, there are other third party apps available in the app store for creating groups on your iPad directly. This can't be done natively and requires such an app to do so. I will go over apps in a variety of categories, including this one, in Chapter 28 entitled, *Covering Your Apps*.

CHAPTER 8

Messages

I Might Actually Enjoy Texting, Once I get the Hang of It

The Messages app was a new feature in iOS 5.0. A combination texting app and instant messaging app, messages can be exchanged between iOS users, and now, Mountain Lion users, Apple's latest OS X (Operating System), free of charge. There may be a charge for internet or wireless usage, of course, but not for the ability to send and/or receive messages.

If you've never "Texted" on your smartphone, or "Chatted" online via Yahoo! Messenger, AOL, or MSN messenger, to name a few, I'll review how this app works. First of all, if you've ever watched or paid attention to your teen children, grandchildren, nieces, or nephews, you'll know that this method of communication has its own language. In the back of this book you'll find a glossary with some of the more commonly used shortcuts and their meanings. I do want to warn you that there are some offensive expressions listed in that section, so be forewarned. Keep in mind, you don't need knowledge of this lingo to communicate well with your friends and loved ones; it just helps shorten the typing process when you use some of those acronyms and other shortcuts. Check out the shortcut glossary and, if you dare, you may find that you can "Speak" to your youngsters in their own language, at least in part. For a more complete listing of messaging shortcuts, check out http://gramtt.us/Ova0ZX online. That site has quite a comprehensive glossary.

Now, for the mechanics of the process. A little practice will enable you to enjoy this form of communication for what it is, a quick and easy way to stay in touch. The first time you use iMessage, the iPad messaging app, it requires a little extra effort. The first step in the process is to go to Settings -> Messages and enable it, or turn it "On." Before you can send or receive messages, you need to set it up by telling it at what address(es) you want to be contacted. In most cases, you'll want to set it up using the email address you commonly use with friends and loved ones in your email communications. To do this, tap the right facing arrow on the "Send & Receive" tab in the "Messages" settings. Enter your apple ID and password, then check off any, or all, the email addresses activated on your iPad that you would like to receive messages using. You can add other email addresses you use by selecting "Add Another Email..." and entering the required address.

In the lower "Send & Receive" section, select the email address you would like to use to send messages from. Additional settings for messaging are the "Send Read Receipts" setting which, when enabled, allows message senders to be notified when you have read their messages, and the "Show Subject Field" setting which, of course, when enabled shows the subject field in messages being sent and when they're received by the recipient. Once your email selections have been verified, you'll be all set to begin "Messaging" on your iPad.

Now, go to the Message app. The first time you may still have to sign in using your Apple id then select which address people should message you at. In cases of iCloud ID there will be @iCloud and @me options available. Select any, or all, then click the blue "Next" button to go on. Your addresses will be verified and you will be taken to the new message page. Note, once this is done in settings, this step may no longer be necessary.

To send a message, enter either the first few letters of your intended recipient's name, email address, or phone number, in the "To" field. If you're not sure how you have that contact listed in your "Contacts" book, tap the plus sign to the right of the "To" box and a list of all of your contacts on your iPad will come from which you can scroll through and select. It is also possible to select more than one contact, if you'd like to send the message to multiple recipients, by again tapping the plus (+) sign and making additional selection(s). Once your recipient(s) have been set, enter your message at the bottom of the column and tap "Send."

If you want to be notified when you receive messages, go to Settings -> Sounds and select a sound for incoming messages. You'll receive a message either on your lock screen, if you're not currently using your iPad, or on your home screen, if you've set it up that way. It can show who it's from and a couple of lines from the message, again depending on your settings. You decide! A notification banner can show on your home screen as a notification with the little bar at the top of the page. To open the message you can either click on the notification bar or, if you miss it, on the message icon.

In the Messaging app, you also have the option of sending a photo with your message.

If you want to send a photo:

1. Tap the Camera Icon to the Left of the Message Field and Select Camera Roll, Photo Stream (if Enabled), or Camera to Take a Picture

2. Add a Message If You Desire, Then Click Send

To Copy Parts of a Thread to Send to Someone

1. Select the Action Icon

2. Select the Parts You Want To Forward

3. Select Forward and Address the Message to Whom You'd Like to Send It

To Delete Messages From a Thread

1. Tap the Action Icon at the Top Right of App

2. Select the Messages You Want to Delete. A Check Mark Will Appear in the Circle to the Left of the Message.

3. Tap Delete

To Delete an Entire Thread

1. Tap the "Edit" Button on the Upper Left of the Thread List

2. Tap the Red Minus Sign to the Left of Persons Name

3. Tap "Delete" to Confirm Delete or Cancel to Exit Action

To Delete All Threads

1. Tap "Clear All" at the Top of the Thread List

To send audio, video, location, or contact information, tap the appropriate icon within the applicable app, generally the right facing arrow in a little box (action icon) in the upper right hand corner of the page, and select "Message." You'll then be prompted to enter your information. Send as instructed above.

CHAPTER 9

Mail, The App

Introduction and Set Up

The settings for the Mail, Contacts, and Calendar apps are under the one umbrella but they are actually three separate programs. We'll go over each in detail but, for now, we'll discuss just the Mail app.

This application did not see a lot of change from iOS 5.1.1 to iOS 6.1. Any changes that might have been made did not leave a large imprint. Now, on with the show!

Overview

The Mail app is a basic featured, but not stripped down, mail client. All of the standard functions, (i.e. compose, reply, forward, delete, etc.), are available plus a few additional, and very useful, features. Let's start at the very beginning with the basic set up.

Set Up

If you've never used the mail app before, there are some preliminary steps that must be employed. First, go to Settings -> Mail, Contacts, Calendar -> Accounts -> Add Account and tap it to select it. If you've set up an account already, and would like to set up a second, third, or whatever, you can follow right along, the procedure is the same. Now, the first time you do this, you should be able to set it up from within the app itself as well; however, for any subsequent email accounts, it must be done through settings as described here.

After tapping Add Account, you will be presented with six named options and an "Other" option. Select the applicable type of account you have. If not listed, select Other. If you have one of the named type of accounts, the process is fairly straightforward. You'll need to enter your name, email address, password for your email account, and, for your own benefit, a description of the account. This really only comes into play if you have several accounts with the same internet service provider (ISP) or mail account provider such as gmail, yahoo.mail, etc. It enables you to keep them separated in your mail account if you want or need to do so. An example of this would be someone who has both a work and a personal gmail account. When mail comes in, you would more than likely want to keep them separated based on the account. If you have named one "Work" and one "Personal," you'll know at a glance which is which. Don't knock yourself out trying to be original because it is strictly for your eyes only.

Once all of the aforementioned information has been entered, tap "Next" on the upper right corner. The Mail app will verify the information and, if all checks out, it will go ahead and set up your account. That's it! You're all done!

If, however, you have an "Other" ISP or mail provider, a little more detail is required. After selecting "Other" you'll be taken to another page where you'll be able to add your mail account, contact information, or calendar. In this chapter on Mail, we'll be selecting Add Mail Account. A New Account window will pop-up. On this page you'll enter the same information described above for the named accounts; i.e., name, email address, password, and description. When all information is entered, it will again be verified. If all checks out, you're all set. Mail will make an effort to determine the pop or IMAP, incoming server, as well as the SMTP or outgoing server. If it's successful you'll have an account all set up from that information.

There are times, though, when Mail is unable to ascertain the necessary information from the data provided. In these cases, a little more research on your part may be necessary. Along with the other details, you'll also need to find out either from your ISP or, in some cases, your home computer, what those incoming and outgoing server settings should be. With all that information, your account will be set up and you'll be in business.

Continue adding accounts in this fashion as often as you'd like. There is no limit to the number of accounts you can add but, with such a small amount of flash storage space, you may prefer to limit it yourself to only those accounts you really need to hear from. I have in the neighborhood of 16 email accounts and I get an awful lot of email each day. I certainly don't want all of that email cluttering up the space on my iPads so I only include three or four of those accounts on my iPad for sanity's sake. Those are the ones I absolutely need to keep up to the minute with. If on my iPad for an extended period of time, I use web mail for the other accounts, checking in periodically to be sure things are running smoothly.

Other Settings

If you look down the Mail, Contacts, Calendars column, you'll see there are several other areas of the Mail app that can be set up and tailored to your particular desires. The first box under the Add Account in the Account section is "Fetch New Data." To the right of that will be the word Push. This is the default setting for your mail delivery. What that means essentially is that, as new mail comes in, you will be immediately notified of it as it is "Pushed" through to your account. If you tap on the right facing arrow to the right of the word Push, you will notice that Push is enabled or turned on. Under the Push switch is a Fetch group of settings. These settings only come into play if Push is disabled or turned off, or for other applications that don't support Push. Those settings give you the option of fetching your mail every 15 minutes, 30 minutes, Hourly, or Manually. Again, if Push is enabled above, these settings do not mean anything as far as the Mail app is concerned.

Under this "Timed" section is an Advanced box with a right facing arrow. Selecting this arrow will allow you to set your accounts individually as far as Push or Fetch settings go. In other words, you can have one mail account Push your mail immediately, and have another Fetch every hour if you'd like. These settings can be completely customized.

Returning to the Mail, Contacts, Calendars column on the first page, you will next come to a "Mail" section. There are several options in this section that you can set up to suit yourself. The first is "Show" and, to the right of that will be a number of recent messages. By default, the setting is 50 Recent Messages. Selecting the arrow to the far right of that box, you'll see that other options are: 100 Recent Messages, 200 Recent Messages, 500 Recent Messages, and 1,000 Recent Messages.

Next in line is "Preview." The default here is two lines. Selecting the arrow on the far right of that box gives you the further options of: None, 1 line, 3 lines, 4 lines, and 5 lines. From there you go to the Show To/Cc Label. This setting can be enabled (turned on) or disabled (turned off). If enabled, all new email going out will have a visible Cc box.

The next option is an important one, especially if all this is new to you. That is the "Ask Before Deleting" option. My suggestion is to enable this setting, or turn it on, so that, before any work in Mail is deleted, it's verified that is in fact what you want to do. It never hurts to be careful and even experienced iPad and Email users will normally avail themselves of this option, including myself.

Load Remote Images is the next option in line. When this is enabled, email images are automatically downloaded when the mail is opened. There are a couple of disadvantages to doing this. First, most of these images are stored on remote servers and downloading these images lets the sender know that you were interested enough in their mail, even junk mail, to take a look. The other disadvantage is, it lets the sender know, not only that you opened the mail, but also your general where-abouts. That's a lot of information to reveal to the sender of junk or even infected mail.

If you have an email account that you keep fairly private and don't receive a lot of email in it, enabling this setting may not be such a bad thing. On the other hand, if it's a fairly well used account, you may not be inclined to reveal so much information about yourself. If the latter is the case, I strongly recommend disabling the Loading of Remote Images.

Next we have "Organize By Thread." Enabling this function will allow Mail to combine correspondence between yourself and another particular individual or entity into groups of email. These threads, as they are known, make for a convenient system of tracking conversations that you've had back and forth with someone over an issue for example. Personally, I like threads a lot and use them both on my Mac and my iPad. If you've never tried it, I recommend doing so for a short time to see how you like the outcome. You, too, may find that it is a convenient method of dealing with matters.

The Final Mail Settings Section

The first option in the final section of Mail settings is "Always Bcc Myself." If you've ever had any office experience, you'll know that a Bcc is a blind carbon copy. It took me a long time to learn this and I had worked in office settings for quite some time before I figured it out. Enabling The Always Bcc Myself setting means that, whenever you send an email, a copy of that email will automatically be sent to you as well. You may wonder why you would ever want to do such a thing. You probably get enough mail and figure it makes no sense to send yourself more. Let me explain why I always enable this setting. When I send out email on my iPad or iPhone, I have no record of that on my Mac or PC. When I have this setting enabled, I no longer have to wonder whether or not I responded to someone's email or whether or not I initiated an email to someone that I've been meaning to write to. I have a copy of that email on all my devices. I set up filters on my Mac that automatically file email from me in a secondary "Sent" folder, so looking back, I can easily find any of this correspondence.

Whether or not you choose to do the same is entirely up to you, but there are definitely some pros and cons to setting it up either way. You'll have to weigh each and decide which way to go.

Next is Increase Quote Level. This is another setting that can be either enabled or disabled. When turned on, this setting will allow you to increase and/or decrease the quote level in your mail messages. If you never want to increase or decrease quote levels, you can just leave this off, but the default setting is on.

Signature is next in line and this line has the well known default "Sent from my iPad" signature message. If you've always wondered where that comes from or what can be done about it, this is where you can change that email ending. You can "sign" your email any way you see fit, and it is not mandatory to have that Apple pre-set message on all of your outgoing messages. Set this as personally as you'd like and you can set it per account or for all accounts. Should you decide to set it per account, tap that option and a box representing each of your existing email accounts will drop down the column. Make your changes accordingly, then change the message in each if you choose to do so.

Finally, we come to the Default Account setting. This is the account that outgoing mail will, by default, be sent from. This can be changed on a case by case basis, but if no alterations are made, mail will be sent from the account displayed here. If you don't want the set account to be your default account, tap the arrow and select the account you'd like. This wraps up Mail settings in the Mail, Contacts, Calendars Settings. There are other Mail related settings to attend to, however.

Notification Mail Settings

From Mail, Contacts, Calendars, we move to the Notifications Settings. Selecting Notifications you will see the Mail app listed as either "In Notification Center" or "Not In Notification Center," depending on what you've set up in the past. If it's not "In," you can select it from the "Not In" section and turn on or enable notifications so that it is placed in the top section. Once Mail notifications are enabled, you can fine tune those notifications by tapping the right facing arrow on the right side of the Mail box. No pun intended.

If you tap that arrow you will be taken to a new page where the first item is Show. The default setting is 5 Unread Items. If you tap the arrow you'll see the other options of 1 unread item, 10 unread items, and 20 unread items. Your selection here will mean that that many items will appear in a notification banner or alert, if they are enabled.

Moving down to the next section, you'll see a box for each of your email accounts. Under that account name will be a word or words indicating what, if any, notifications you've enabled for each account. For each account that you want notifications enabled, tap the little right facing arrow and another new page will open up. On this new page you can:

◆ Turn Notification Center on or off;

◆ Select your preferred alert style; i.e., None, Banners, or Alerts;

- ◆ Enable or disable the Badge App Icon (this is the little blue "Badge" on an icon with a number on it which indicates how many items in that app need your attention);

- ◆ Select a new mail sound, if any;

- ◆ Choose whether or not a preview of the message will appear with the notification in Notification Center; and

- ◆ Choose whether these notifications will appear on your lock screen or not.

This can be done for each mail account on your iPad. If the badges, or red emblems on top of the icons, aggravate you or nag you too much, take heart, you can just disable them right here! Some students have indicated they really like this feature because they know exactly where they stand before opening up the Mail app, while others are plain miffed at it because it's just another reminder of all they've got to do. It seems like it's a loved or hated feature and there aren't too many neutral views on it. Whatever your situation, make your adjustments here then we'll move on to sending mail.

Keeping Up With Correspondence

Viewing Your Messages

One of the first things you'll likely want to do once your account is set up, other than check your mail, is write to a friend or loved one. To do either, tap the Mail icon. If you have unread mail, you may notice that there is a red "badge" on the icon with a number on it. That number indicates how many unread email you currently have in your inbox. These notifications or badges, as they are known, can be enabled and/or disabled as described in the prior section so, going beyond that feature, once the Mail icon is tapped the app should open to an account page or your inbox.

If you find yourself on an account page, a page listing all of your folders or mailboxes, just select your Inbox to view your mail. If, instead, you're already in your Inbox, you'll know because there will be a panel on the left side of your screen with the location named "Inbox" across the center of the top of that column. There will be a left facing arrow to the left of it if you have other mail accounts. That arrow will be directing you back to the account page I've just described. To the right on top of that column will be the word "Edit" in a dark grey button. More about that in a few minutes.

To read a mail item in your inbox, tap the item listed and the body of the email should show up on the right of your screen. Depending on who your server or ISP (Internet Service Provider) is, the column may move completely out of your way, giving you a full screen view of the applicable email item. After reading it, to return to your inbox, tap the dark grey box on the upper left of your screen where it will say Inbox or the name of the last page you were on. For example, if you were in your Inbox, that grey block will say Inbox and may have a number next to it indicating how many unread mail items you currently have. If you have multiple mail accounts, you have the option of going to "All Inboxes" to view your mail from all of your accounts simultaneously. If that's where you were prior to opening up the mail item you're currently reading, that upper grey box will say "All Inboxes."

Now, again depending on who your ISP is, you may also see an up and a down arrow to the right of the box name that you are in. If you do, you can choose to scroll through your mail via those arrows. The up arrow would take you to the newest email item and the down arrow would take you to the one received immediately prior to the one you're currently on. Also, depending on your ISP, there may be a couple of numbers in the center top of your mail item. For example, it may say 156 of 249, as mine does at this moment. That indicates that you are currently on mail item 156 out of a total of 249. Now, you may wonder why I keep saying, "Depending on your ISP" but all are different. GMail accounts sometimes show something differently from an AOL account which may show something different from an iCloud account. With such diversity in internet service providers and email providers, it's no wonder that things may be a little different from one type of account to another.

No matter who your provider, though, the overall structure will be the same, even if the details aren't. You should have an inbox no matter who your provider is. There should be a left column once your inbox is selected from your account page. You will open your email by selecting it from the inbox panel. And, of course, you will read it the same way! There are times when you may have difficulty viewing your email because the inbox column didn't retract out of sight when you selected the message. If that's the case, sometimes shifting the orientation from portrait to landscape, or vice versa, assists with that. If all else fails, give it a try.

Just a note here to let you know the blue dot in front of some emails in your inbox indicates that is an unread message. Another question I'm frequently asked is why deleting mail on your iPad doesn't remove it from your inbox on your computer and vice versa. The answer is no, removing from one will not remove it from another, you have to delete it on both. If you were deleting it from a web mail account prior to its download, it would be deleted from both, but making the change in your device's mail client won't do it.

Responding to Mail

Upon reading a mail message, you may decide you'd like to respond to that message or send it on to a friend for them to review. You will see, on the top right hand side of your screen, there are several little icons up there. To reply or forward your message, we'll work with the left facing curved arrow, which normally is the second from the right.

Tapping that arrow will open a drop-down box with several options. You will see: Reply; Reply All; Forward; Save Image or Video, if one or the other is included in the message; and Print. Choose the applicable option, either Reply, Reply All, or Forward. If you choose Reply, a new message will come up already addressed to the person that sent the message you are replying to. If you chose Reply All, you'll see all the applicable names in the To and CC/BCC fields. The subject will be "Re:" whatever the original subject was. And the cursor will be all set on the top of the message ready for you to just enter your response. When you're done typing your message, just tap "Send" to send it off, or "Cancel" if you've changed your mind. If you've changed your mind before entering any text, the reply message will just slide back down to where it came from and no harm done. If you've entered any text into the reply message, when you click "Cancel" you'll have an option to save or delete the draft. This is always how you save "Drafts" when you'd like to work on something later that you've already begun. Just tap "Save Draft" and it will be in your "Drafts" folder on your account page. If, on the other hand, you know you won't want to send what you've written, just select "Delete Draft" and your work won't be saved.

If you'd like to forward your message to your lawyer or someone else, select "Forward" from the drop-down box that comes up when you tap that left facing arrow at the top of the page. If there were any attachments included in the email you're forwarding, a message will immediately come up asking if you want to include or not include those attachments in your forwarded message. Generally, that's where the evidence, (er, I mean information) in question, is - sorry about that. Select your choice there, and the message will come up with the cursor in the To field, ready for you to enter the name of the person to whom you want to forward this message. To the far right of the cursor, there will be a little white plus (+) sign in a blue circle. Should you want to send this to more than one person, tap that plus (+) sign and a list of all your contacts will come up with a search box at the top with the cursor in it all ready for you. You'll also notice, if you have contacts stored in Groups on your iPad, that there is a "Groups" button on the upper left of the pop up panel. If you want to send it to a "Formal" group of people that you have stored in your contacts, tap the Groups button and a list of all of your groups in your iPad contacts will come up. If you choose one group, the members of that group will come up upon tapping Done. Select to whom from among that list you would like to send this message and their name will magically appear in the To field with the cursor to the right of it, ready for your next entry. Amazing little gadgets aren't they?!

Assuming you're done entering your intended recipients, tap the space in the email message above the message in question and type in any message you may choose to add to it, then proceed as instructed above by either sending or canceling your forward.

Composing New Messages

If reading an incoming message prompts you to want to write your own, or at any other time for that matter, you will want to create something from scratch. To do so, select the little piece of paper with a writing instrument on it to the far right at the top of the page. A new, blank email will pop up and the cursor will be in position for you to enter the name of the person to whom you wish to send the message. Again there'll be a plus (+) sign to the far right which will work the same as described above in "Responding to Mail."

If you've chosen to always Bcc yourself as we discussed in setting up your mail accounts, you will see that the Cc/Bcc field is visible and your name will be filled in after the word From. Next, you should always enter a subject if you want to be sure your message will get read. Many people these days set up their spam filters to discard any messages coming in without a clear subject field. Even if it does make it past the recipient's spam filters, it always seems polite to me to let them know why it is that you've decided to write to them. In this day and age when people are inundated with email, many prioritize their email reading based on subject matter. With the most important dealt with first. If your message isn't even important enough to have a subject, it may not make it through this next step or, at the very least, not quickly.

Without further belaboring the point, I recommend always having a subject filled in unless you're very close to the recipient and know that any message from you will be handled promptly. After the subject, tap the message field to set your cursor in there and begin entering the body of your message. Interestingly enough, as a test, I didn't enter a recipient's name or address, the subject, and only typed xyz in the body of an email. By entering "xyz" the Send button was enabled, I selected Send and received an error message that there was no subject and asking if I wanted to send it anyway. I chose Send again and, lo and behold, it was sent, without a recipient or an error message. Interesting little test I thought, you probably just think I'm crazy sending an email to no one with no message, no subject, and Cc'ing myself. Oh well, such is the life of a scientist or a techie!

At any rate, assuming you're actually planning on sending a message to somebody for some purpose - the mechanics of sending and/or canceling are identical to those of replying and forwarding. You can Send, Cancel, and Save or Delete the Draft.

Sending Photos

A new, and very nice, feature in iOS 6.0, and later, is the ability to now send photos from within the Mail app itself. Prior to this release, attaching, or enclosing photos, had to be done from within the Photo app instead. This was counter-intuitive for most iOS users as well as bothersome. You couldn't just write up, or respond to, an email and, as an afterthought, include an image from your iPad's photo library.

Now, if you'd like to include an image in an email, all you have to do is tap and hold the place in the message that you would like to insert your image. Several options will pop up, one of which is "Insert Photo or Video." Select this option from the pop up menu, choose your image source (Usually Camera Roll), then select your desired image.

The image will appear in the position you set and all you have to do is complete your message and send it.

There are times when, if you include an image that was taken by another device, you'll see the word "Image" in the upper right hand side of the screen, next to the Subject field. That word will be followed by a size in kilobytes or megabytes (Mb), depending on the size of the image. When this information is provided, you may note that the file size of the image is greater than that allowed by your email provider for attachments. If this is the case, tap on the word Image and another pop up will appear. You'll be presented with several sizing options in descriptive words, such as: Smaller, Medium, Actual Size, and Larger. To resize the image so that it complies with your provider's requirements, just select a size from the pop up menu. As you change image sizes, you will see the image actually become smaller, or larger, whatever the case may be, right before your eyes. The file size will change in relationship to the image size so that you'll know exactly what you're doing. When you've adjusted to the required size, you can go ahead and send it. When adjusting the size, don't worry about going too small or too large, initially, because it can be resized immediately with no ill effects.

Other Attachments

Sending other types of attachments, such as documents, that were created in other apps, remains the same as in iOS 5.1.1. Any other type of attachment, other than photos, has to be sent from within the app it was created in. Not all apps provide this feature but most do. Even photos can be sent from within the photo app itself, should you choose to do so while viewing your image library.

Open the app in question, select the desired attachment, and look for the sharing button within the app. Generally, the share button is the same within most apps. It is a little action button, right facing arrow or right facing arrow coming out of a box, in most cases. If you don't see a share button within the app, you may not be able to send the document via email or any other source. As an alternative, if you can't share from within the app itself, you may find that you can save the document to iCloud, DropBox, Box.net, or some other online storage solution from which you would be able to share it. Short of this, there is always the possibility that, from within iTunes on your computer, the app has a file sharing option. Go to the Apps tab within iTunes, when your iPad is selected in the left column under Devices. Scroll to the bottom of the Apps page to the "File Sharing" section and look for the desired app. If it's listed there, select it and any documents currently on your iPad within that app will be listed. Select the document and click on "Save To," and select the location you'd like to save the document to. If you're unfamiliar with the directory set up on your computer, the simplest thing is to save it to your desktop. From there you can include it as an attachment from an email generated from your computer's mail client. A little convoluted, but it gets the job done nonetheless.

Other Options

Icon Upon Icon

Returning briefly to the right facing arrow coming out of a box, or the action button. Let's discuss a couple of other options in there. I believe we spoke about the "Save Image" or "Save Video" options if there are images or videos in the applicable email message. All you have to do is select that option to copy then paste your image elsewhere in another document or wherever else you'd like.

The Print option, also in the drop-down from that action button, is probably one of the most crucial options in most apps. Most of my students want to know how they can print their documents and photos from their iPad. Throughout this book we'll discuss printing options with your iPad but, at this point, the easy answer is that you should have an AirPrint compatible printer to print natively from your iPad. To do so, select Print. A window will pop up asking you to select your printer. If you've never printed from it before, it will then search for any AirPrint compatible printers on your Wi-Fi network and list them in that window. Select the one you'd like to use then select the number of copies and, if your printer does duplex printing, whether or not you want it printed on both sides. Then tap Print, and you're all set. If you don't have an AirPrint compatible printer, we'll be discussing other options later in the book, so don't fret.

Moving a little beyond simply sending and receiving email, you'll see there are a series of icons at the upper right of your mail when in reading mode. There was another option in the left facing arrow icon but we'll come back to that in a minute. To the left of the arrow you'll see either a trash can or a box, again depending on who your mail account is with.

If you have the box to the left of the arrow, after tapping it you'll see an "Archive Message" option. Archiving a message would place it into an archive folder in your mail account. Some people like to do this to organize their mail, they'll place older mail messages that they won't need to access as often in this folder. We'll look at that folder in a minute.

If you have a trash can to the left of the arrow, you could tap that to discard the open message. Depending on how you've set up your mail account, this action may or may not be confirmed prior to the action being completed. We spoke a little about that when we covered settings earlier in this book. If you decide to trash a message, it doesn't delete it completely from your iPad. Like your deleted mail on your computer, all deleted mail goes directly into a deleted folder in your mail account. We'll also look at that folder in a minute.

If you would rather have a "Trash" option at the top of your open mail than an "Archive" option, you can change this in settings. If you have a Gmail account, you may, by default, have the "Archive" folder and option rather than the "Trash" option. To change this default setting, go to Settings -> Mail, Contacts, Calendars -> "Your Account Name," where "Your Account Name" is the name of your account. Tap the arrow on the right side of that box and go down to "Archive Messages." Now turn it off, or disable it, click Done and you're all set! You will now have a trash can at the top of your open mail page instead of the archive box. That simple! You may have to change messages to see the results but don't worry, you will have done what needed to be done and the change will be immediate.

To the left of the "Trash" can, is a folder icon with a down arrow in it. Tapping this icon will bring up a listing of your accounts on the left side of your page. What you've done is invoke the "Move" action and your Mail app is waiting for you to tell it to which folder you wish to move the message in question. Don't panic, you can change your mind and just tap "Cancel." No harm done. Remember what I said. There's very little you can do that can't be undone simply enough with a little know-how. By the end of this book, you'll have the know-how to set things straight yourself.

The fifth, and final, icon on the upper right, above your mail message, is a flag. Selecting this icon will enable you to either "flag," or mark, your email as important or as unread. Many people choose to flag their messages for one reason or another. On your computer, your mail client probably gives you a choice of about five different flag colors to use. You can select a color to depict a variety of circumstances; i.e., Important, Needs Reply, Reread, etc. Unfortunately, the Mail app on your iPad only has one color for coding and that is red. Should you choose to flag any messages, they'll all be "flagged" the same, with a red flag.

If you glance at your "Inbox" listing on the left of your screen in Mail, you'll notice that some messages may have a blue dot to the left of them in the list, while others don't. The reason for this is, in all likelihood, you've opened, or read, the messages without the dot. Only messages that are unread, or unopened (your iPad can't distinguish between you merely "Opening" and actually "Reading" a message), have a blue dot to the left of them in the inbox listing. As soon as a message is next in line to be read as you go down the inbox column, that message is opened, whether you take the time to read it then or not. At times, you may get up to a message but have to leave it and want to come back to it. In such an instance, you may decide to "Mark As Unread" so that you remember to come back to that message to read it later. Alternately, once a message has been marked as unread, you may decide to mark it as read so you don't go back to it again. You can "Unflag" and "Mark as Read" once they have been marked as flagged and/or unread. Any of the above actions can be done by using the flag icon and selecting the applicable option.

Moving Into Your Accounts Inboxes

We've now covered the basic options in reading and writing email, so we'll move to more of an overall picture of the process. From your inbox, you'll notice that there is a left pointing arrow/button on the upper left of your inbox column that may say, depending on where you are, "Mailbox" - if you have several accounts and are in one particular, it may indicate the name of your main account. Selecting this button will take you back to the main account pages in Mail.

Again, if you have more than one account, you'll see a list of the various accounts that are set up on your iPad. The upper section of this column will be for "Inboxes" and the lower section for "Accounts." Additionally, if you have several accounts, the uppermost box in the "Inbox" section will be "All Inboxes." To the right of that box will be a number in a grey circle, and then a right facing arrow. Needless to say, the arrow will take you back into the inbox we just came from, The number, on the other hand, indicates how many unread messages you have in that particular inbox.

Under the "All Inboxes" will be a "VIP" box. New since iOS 6.0, the VIP box enables you to include special people from whom, for whatever reason, it is important for you to know when you receive mail and whose mail you would like to keep separate from others. If you tap the VIP box, you will see an option to add VIPs. If you tap that option, a list of all the "Groups" in your contacts will open up. If you have no other groups in your contacts, but back up to iCloud, there will be an option for the iCloud group. If, in fact, you have groups in addition to your regular contacts, those groups will also be listed here. Select a group that the contacts you want to add are in, then select Done in the upper right side of the column. A full listing of all contacts in that group will come up. On a one-by-one basis, select each of the contacts you want to be VIP's. After each selection, tap the "Add VIP" button until you've included everyone you would like to add. If you've listed everyone in a group that you'd like to add, but there are additional people in another group, once you've selected Done again, a listing of all the groups will again appear. Continue adding in this fashion until you're completely satisfied with the list, then select Done a final time. Now, all mail that you had in your inboxes from the VIPs will be moved over to this new inbox, automatically. If you later add a contact that you also want to add to your VIP list, you will be able to do so at that time, so you're not locked in to the selections you've just made to the exclusion of all others.

Finally in the inbox section, if you've flagged any mail, you will also have an inbox for flagged mail. If you'll remember, this is mail that, for whatever reason, you wanted to mark as special. Here Mail keeps it in a special place for you to see. Note that, although your VIP and flagged mail are now separated from the others, they will still be in the "All Inboxes" inbox as well.

The Accounts Section

Moving down into the account section, will reveal some new territory in Mail. Once again, you'll see a listing of each of your accounts in Mail with the number of unread email reflected in a grey circle to the right of the account name. However, should you tap the right facing arrow on the right of the named account box, you may find some interesting things, again depending on who your mail provider is.

Gmail accounts have a plethora of folders from which to choose. Many IMAP accounts are similar in their set-up to these Gmail accounts. If, on the other hand, you simply have a POP account, and I'm talking about the incoming server settings which we dealt with at the beginning of this chapter, these may or may not have been automatically filled in for you as would be the case with Gmail account set-ups. In these cases, you may be totally unaware of whether your incoming server is POP or IMAP or any other acronym you might imagine. But these are the two basic incoming server types and most mail falls into one or the other category.

If you have a POP incoming server setting, in all likelihood, you simply have "Inbox" when you select the arrow to the right of the named account. Selecting this inbox will take you to exactly the same place as selecting the same inbox from the "Inbox" section. You can verify which type you have, if it was automatically set up for you by Mail, by going to Settings -> Mail, Contacts, Calendars -> "Account," where account is the name of your particular account. Tap the right facing arrow to the right of the box and a box will pop up with the incoming mail server settings filled in. On the "Host Name" line, the first box in that section, you will see either pop or IMAP preceding a series of initials which represent your email providers domain settings. That's the easiest way to know which you've got if you think you should have some boxes that you don't currently have.

In Gmail accounts and some other IMAP accounts, you'll find some or all of the following folders in addition: Drafts, Sent Mail, Spam,

Trash, All Mail, Important, Starred, Deleted Messages, and any other folders you may have personally added to this account. In the Gmail web mail account, you can mark as Important and Star various messages. The same is true in the Gmail iPad app. If you've done that through either route, the applicable marked messages will be in their proper folders.

The other folders more or less speak for themselves. You will notice that each one will have a number next to it, if there are unread messages in them, indicating the number of included, unread messages. If you look at the upper right side of IMAP account columns, you will see an "Edit" button. Tapping this button will allow you to "Add" an additional folder or, as it's referred to here, "Mailbox" within a mailbox to the account in question. Again, this is only with IMAP accounts. Precluding POP accounts from adding folders is not an Apple decision, it is a restriction of POP accounts in general. It is not a matter of Apple being exclusionary in their treatment of this type of incoming server.

Moving and Deleting Mail

More Than One Way

We already spoke a little about the option of moving mail by tapping the folder icon with the down arrow from the upper right side of your messages. We also discussed deleting messages by selecting the little trash can icon to its right. But there's more than one way to skin a cat, and so it is with moving and deleting mail in the Mail app.

If we go back to our inboxes and select any inbox, you should be back to the inbox list of messages. Along with being able to delete, or in some cases archive (if you haven't changed those accounts that archive instead of deleting yet, as detailed in the previous section), by tapping the applicable icon at the upper right of your message. For this example, we'll discuss the delete option and assume that all you archivers out there have decided you'd rather trash your old mail than archive it. Another way to delete messages, in addition to the trash can icon, is to go to the message in the inbox column and swipe, with one finger, from right to left on the listed message. A red delete button should appear. You can then select that button to delete as well. If you have the archive option instead, the same will hold true for you but replace delete with archive in these instructions. (See Figure 1 and Figure 2)

Notice that, while you have that little red delete button in the inbox list, the Edit button at the top right of the column becomes a Done button. If you've changed your mind about deleting the message, you can either reverse swipe, or swipe from left to right, or you can tap the Done button at the top and no delete or archive action will take place. Note, if you have questionable email messages, and aren't sure whether they may be viruses or not, you can delete them, before they're actually opened, in this manner. In doing so, you could be avoiding a potential mess. I know Apple products are supposed to be pretty much immune to this type of attack, but there's always an exception to a circumstance and you don't want to be that exception so, if they're called for, implement safety precautions.

Figure 1 - While Reading an Email, You'll See a Trash Can Icon at the Top of the Page. Tap It to Delete.

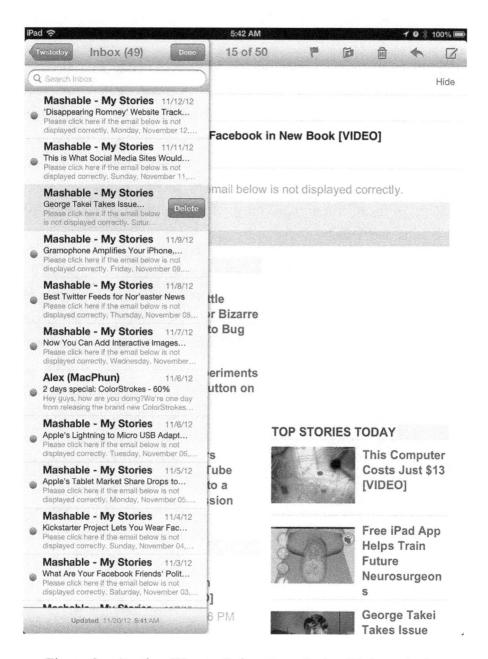

Figure 2 - Another Way to Delete Is to Swipe Right to Left on a Message Listed in Your Inbox.

More Than Two Ways

You may be in a similar situation to the one I'm in and have several, or many whatever the case may be, email messages that are junk and need to be deleted. Don't get me wrong, I read all legitimate messages that come to me from individuals, but there are many messages that are simply advertising or spamming and I dismiss them without a second glance. If this is your situation as well, there is a way to dismiss several messages at once with no need for the back and forth slow actions of one-by-one deletions.

If you go back to the Inbox column and select the Edit button on the upper right, you'll see the column visually changes. The message listings move to the right somewhat in the column and an empty circle opens up to the left of each message listed. To delete multiple messages, go along and select the messages you choose not to keep by tapping anywhere on the applicable message in the column. Continue selecting, even scrolling down further if you so choose, until all messages you want to handle are selected. Now, go to the bottom of the column and select the appropriate action. In this instance it would be Delete, but notice there are two other options available as well. You may decide to just Move the selected messages to another account or mailbox. Or, you may choose to Mark the messages as Read or Unread, whatever the case may be. But, note, you can't take any action until at least one message is selected in the list. The options are all "greyed" out until a message is selected upon which to act. (See Figure 3). Don't worry, if you've changed your mind after selecting several email, just tap the "Cancel" button at the top of the column and, no harm, no foul!

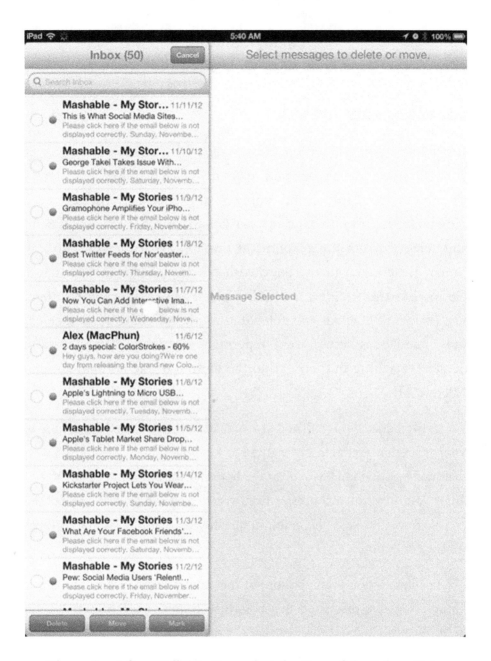

Figure 3 - After "Edit" Is Tapped at the Top of the Inbox Column, Options on the Bottom of the Column Are Greyed Out Until a Message Is Selected for Action.

Finally Deleting

Cleaning Up After Yourself

Just like on your Computer, trash is not fully deleted from any of your IMAP accounts when you select delete. You must periodically go to your trash folder and empty it to permanently delete these old messages. To do so, go to your Gmail, or other IMAP account, and select it from the accounts at the bottom of the left column. You will be taken to the page with all of your mailboxes listed. Go to your trash folder, tap "Edit" in the upper right corner, then, just like you did when you deleted multiple messages earlier, select those messages that you want to permanently delete. If you want to delete everything in there, go to the bottom of the column and tap "Delete All."

If, by chance, you realize that you inadvertently placed a message in your trash that you actually wanted to keep in another mailbox, select that message and tap "Move" at the bottom of the column. A listing of all of your inboxes will appear from which you can choose. Select the box you want to keep the email in question in and it'll be placed there for further action.

The last option at the bottom of the column, while in edit mode, is "Mark." We've discussed this before so I won't go into detail again here. Just think about the fact that if a message is important enough to mark, you may not want it in your trash in the first place. The safest thing to do is to move it to another folder, out of harm's way, until you can act on it.

Wrap Up

Other than letting you know that, when you open your Mail app, that will generally touch off your "Fetching" of email. To fetch mail, pull down slightly on the lower left column until you see a spinner on top. We spoke about that earlier in Mail, Contacts, Calendars settings. You'll know that Mail is "processing" in one of two ways and, sometimes, both ways. First and foremost, there will be a little spinner above the lower left hand column and, when it is bringing in mail, there will be a little progress bar to the right of it that may or may not indicate how many incoming messages you have..

The second way is a more general way. When many apps are processing, you'll see another spinner in the top left side of your screen, next to your wireless indicator. This is tantamount to the hour glass spinner on a PC or a spinning "beach ball" on a Mac. As annoying as those indicators may be when you're waiting for them, they simply indicate that your device is doing its job. With that we'll leave the Mail app.

CHAPTER 10

Safari

Surfing Safari

Anyone for the Beach Boys?!

O K, I'm sorry but as an old and very big fan, I couldn't resist. This is where we talk about a very different kind of "Surfing Safari," and I won't ask you to sing along. All right, now that I've gotten that out of my system, let's talk about the Safari app on your iPad.

If you've done, or want to do, any internet research or other kind of web viewing, you'll need to become familiar with Safari, or another browser. There are several Safari alternatives which we'll discuss when we get to Chapter 28 on third party apps but, for now we'll concentrate on Safari. If coming over from a Mac, and sometimes even a PC, you'll be aware of this browser and what it has to offer. Although the mobile Safari is somewhat different than its full featured, big brother, many still believe it is among the top web browsers available today. Whether that's true or not, in many ways the mobile version leaves a lot to be desired, depending on what you want to do with it.

If all you do is comparison shop, do research, and perform very basic web surfing duties, then it does a stellar job. If you're expecting a little more out of a browser, like viewing online flash videos or sometimes even social networking, you may want to skip ahead to Chapter 28.

What Safari Does

What Safari does do, it does very well. Try to say that three times, quickly. But I believe that's a very fair assessment. In iOS 6.0, the address bar in Safari took on more responsibilities than its predecessor. With iOS 6.0 came full Facebook integration throughout all the iOS built in apps, and that includes Safari. If in your browsing, you find a page worth sharing, just tap the action button at the top (the box with the right facing arrow) and do so via Twitter, Facebook, Email, or iMessage. Once you select your avenue of choice, the applicable web page will be "Attached" or "Linked" to your message.

Also new since iOS 6.0, selecting the action button invokes a little box pop up with icons. Prior to iOS 6.0, this was merely a drop-down list. In my humble opinion, IMHO for you instant messengers, this visual form of communication is much easier on these old eyes than the old list set up. If you take a minute to check out this pop up, you'll see other functions such as Copy, Bookmark, Add to Reading List (also new in iOS 6.0), Print, and Add to Home Screen. Copy is pretty straightforward. If you'd like to make a copy of a page to paste into another document for some reason, or for any reason, just select the Copy option and you'll be in business.

Bookmark, if you've never used Safari before, or many other browsers for that matter, you may not know that a Bookmark is the same as a Favorite. If you want to be able to come back to a page again, you can bookmark it by selecting that option. You'll be presented with an Add Bookmark box. The name of the bookmark will be filled in already, but the cursor will be there for you to make any desired changes. The second line of the Add Bookmark box will have the URL, short for Uniform Resource Locator. In plain English, this is the address that you would need to go to that page again in the future. The final field is Bookmarks. Selecting this will open up a Bookmarks dropdown which will include all of your bookmark folders for organization. You can select any one of these locations to save your bookmark in. If you don't know what you're doing, or don't have a system set up yet, the simplest thing to do would be to just save it as a bookmark, the default location, and it will appear whenever you bring up your bookmarks. If you're more experienced or an orderly sort, the most common folders are Popular, for frequently used sites, and News, for informational sites. The Bookmark Bar is the line immediately under the address bar on your Safari page. If you have any named sources going across this area of your screen, you have a bookmarks bar. An example of this would be: Google Maps, Yahoo!, Evernote, etc. As this list grows, it becomes scrollable. If you want to start off on the right track and become and stay organized, you can go to the little book icon at the top of the page, to the left of the action button, and select it. A drop-down will appear and there will be an Edit button on the top right of the column. Tap Edit and the list will shift to the right and any folders or bookmarks you've added, will have a white minus (-) sign in a red circle to the left of them. To delete them, tap the minus sign. A red delete button, similar to the one in several other apps, will appear on the right side of the selected mark or folder, to delete the mark or folder in question, just tap the delete button. If you've changed your mind, you can tap the minus sign again and the delete button will disappear.

Where the Edit button was at the top when you selected it, you will now see a Done button. To the left of the Bookmarks column is a New Folder button. Here's where you become orderly and create folders that make sense to you. You can clean up what's already there by deleting the old and creating new. Just be aware that, if you've bookmarked pages in the past and placed them in a folder, you can't delete the folder without also deleting the bookmark that's in it.

At the bottom of the Bookmark column you'll see a book icon which, by default, is selected, and a clock icon, indicating your web browsing history by date is stored there, and a pair of glasses. This indicates, what else but, web pages you've added to your reading list. This is a nice feature of Safari which enables you to view webpages you didn't have a chance to read at one time, at another time. I believe in the end, Apple would like these pages to even be available when offline but, as of this writing, that hasn't happened yet. There are other apps available, which will again be covered in the Covering Your Apps chapter, that are available for offline perusal and are presented in a nice, clean and uncluttered fashion. The jury is still out on what Apple will ultimately end up with here but, the competition is stiff.

This all brings us down to the last two icons in the action drop-down, Print and Add to Home Screen. Let's talk first about Print. This is a feature in which many of you are very interested. In order to print from your iOS device, you need an AirPrint compatible printer. Many of the newer Wi-Fi models are AirPrint capable and they're not necessarily expensive peripherals. I've paid $59 for two different, new, Wi-Fi and AirPrint compatible printers which also duplex, or print on both sides of the paper. These are all very desirable features to me and, although they've both been on sale when purchased, this type of deal is not unheard of. On the contrary, they're fairly common these days. You may find, as I have, that it cost more to replace the ink cartridges than to replace the printer, which has been the reason behind two of my printer purchases of late.

Now, if you don't want to spring for a new printer, no matter what the cost, don't despair. There are apps available, "Yes, we'll discuss them later," that allow you to print from any printer from your iOS device whether it's wired or Wi-Fi. Let me explain, here, my reason for putting off the app discussion for one particular chapter. I could be piece-mealing these various apps for you but, when you're done with this book, you'll have no idea where to find the information again. If I consolidate it and put it all in one succinct chapter, it'll be a better point of reference for the future. Listen to grandma, she knows best! OK, so maybe not always but don't tell my children and grandchildren that for heaven's sake!

I've assumed, hopefully rightfully so, that if you really need to know the name of the app right away, you'll skip to the "Covering Your Apps" chapter and take a peek. You can always mark your place and come back to this when you've gotten that answer.

A Neat Little Trick

The final icon in the action drop-down panel is Add to Home Screen. This Apple lovingly refers to as web clips. If you frequent a page on the internet - say a shopping site, social networking site, etc. - you can select this option and an icon with an image of the page in question, will be placed on your home screen. In the future, when you want to visit that site, just tap the icon on your home screen and you'll be immediately taken to that page in Safari. Very handy! Nice little feature, Apple.

What Else Is New?

There were several other new and very nice features added to Safari in iOS 6.0. One of my favorites is called "Reader." Reader shows as a little, greyed out purple box in the address bar of Safari, to the left of the refresh button, or semi-circle with an arrow on the extreme right in the address bar. If you select "Reader" while on a web page, the page will come up in an uncluttered way, no ads, just clean, relative images and text, nothing to distract you in any way. The only other thing than the story itself, are two little letter A's, one smaller than the other. Selecting the A's will bring up a letter sizing option for your reading ease. Note, once you select the Reader button in the address bar, it turns a true purple to indicate that you have Reader open. Also, it takes a few minutes, even on a Wi-Fi connection, to save the article for later reading.

iCloud is another new icon on the Safari page. Situated between the action icon and the bookmark icon you'll see a little cloud icon. Selecting that icon will bring up iCloud Tabs. In other words, iCloud magically shows you all of the tabs you have open on your other iCloud enabled devices. This is very handy if, for example, you need to leave your desktop computer to go to work but want to be able to pick up where you left off as soon as you get to the subway. This feature will do just the trick.

Another of my favorite new features in Safari's iOS 6.x version is the fact that there seems to be no end to the number of tabs you can have open simultaneously. At this moment in time, I have 18 open and counting. Although I haven't tried to go any farther, it seems there would be few, if any, circumstances under which you would need more than that open. If you do, give it a try. You might decide to give it a try anyway. To get to more than the seventh (7th) of these tabs, tap the little double right facing arrow in the tab on the far right. Just remember that having all those web pages open at the same time has a similar effect to having a lot of apps open at the same time, it slows down the processing ability of your iPad. I suspect that's why it's taking so long to save a Reader page to my reading list. Oh well, what we don't do in the name of research!

Oh, by the way, to close those tabs, just tap the little black "x" on the left side of the tab in question. And, if you still want to open more, just tap the little plus (+) sign all the way to the right of the tabs.

Looking Around

If we look a little closer at the Safari app, you'll see that on the upper right side, as in the desktop version of a variety of browsers, there's a search bar in which to initiate a search with Google and other search engines. If you don't know a URL, just enter what you do know about a site in that box and Google will find some suitable options for you. Just a little aside, if you do know the URL, or web address, don't use the search box, use the address bar directly. You'll immediately go to the applicable web page instead of being taken to a search page with several options from which to choose. Of course, if you've got time to spare, don't worry about it, just go ahead and use the search bar anyway. Personally, I get antsy and want to go where I want to go as soon as I can get there. Do not pass go, do not collect $200. Just take me there, right away!

Also, looking all the way to the upper left of the page, you'll find the forward and back arrows which bring you, strangely enough, either forward or backward from where you currently are. I'll say no more on that, I think most of you are familiar with that concept, both experienced and inexperienced. I will say, though, that there are times when, especially in financial activities such as making purchases, you don't want to hit that back arrow or you'll re-purchase whatever you just purchased. In these situations, if you want to go back to where you were prior to checking out, look for a back arrow on the web page itself or, use one of the site's tabs to get to where you want to go. I've had desktop Safari re-order from a store by freezing and needing to be refreshed. I hadn't navigated away from the purchase page yet when it froze and, as soon as it refreshed, the order went through again. Not a good experience, especially when, as in the situation I was in, the merchant doesn't want to cancel the second, identical order without a processing charge. Live and learn. I never did business with that merchant again and always try to immediately leave a page when a purchase is completed.

On that note, I believe we've covered Safari pretty thoroughly. Remember, if you have any questions, feel free to contact me through my site http://GrandmaTalksTech.com.

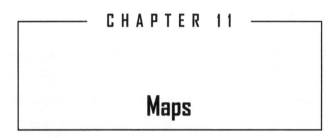

CHAPTER 11

Maps

The Maps App

In iOS 6.0

The Maps app has undergone a lot of revisions, fine tuning, and added features since iOS 6.0. Since this update, Maps now offer "Fly Over" satellite viewing. Users can zoom into a location and get a bird's eye view of the topography. In city viewing, it is possible to survey the street level structures, get a "Fix" on a particular location on the map, and familiarize themselves with the area before ever visiting the location in person.

Gone are the Google Maps, the iPad Maps app has replaced them with Apple's own version. Navigational apps will be able to integrate with the app and provide turn by turn spoken directions. The Maps app, itself, provides its own turn by turn directions but they are only spoken in the Wi-Fi and 4G Model of the iPad 3 and 4, and other Siri enabled iPads that may come along. With Siri, the iPad 3 and later, and iOS 6.0 and later, users can request directions from Siri but, again, she'll only orally give them to you on the 4G model, but will do so even if you're on Wi-Fi with that model. The reason for this has to do with the built in GPS in the 3G and 4G models.

All in all, as you'll see in the following pages, the Maps app revisions are pretty spectacular having been one of the major undertakings of Apple in this new mobile operating system. In this revision, the procedure for using this app has changed somewhat, too, but, for those of you coming from iOS 5.x, it shouldn't be difficult to adjust.

In addition to those new features pointed out in the previous section, the Maps app can provide directions, traffic reports, satellite imagery, street maps, and it can send your exact location to whomever you choose. If you tap a link to a map in other apps on your iPad, the Maps app will open, showing you the location.

Finding Yourself - The View May Be Wonderful

Triangulation

The Wi-Fi /3G or Wi-Fi /4G models Use GPS, while the Wi-Fi models use something called "Triangulation," to pinpoint your location in the iPad's Map App. Most of us are familiar with GPS and have a basic sense of how that works via satellite; however, triangulation may be a little bit different concept so I'll take a moment to give you a brief overview of what it is.

Triangulation is a method of acquiring locations by calculating the amount of time a signal takes to bounce between a minimum of two and, ideally, three points. In so doing, a relative distance can be determined from each thereby placing the source of that signal in the center and pinpointing, fairly accurately, someone's exact location.

An excellent example of triangulation at work is the following given by qrg.northwestern.edu:

> *Hikers can use radio waves to triangulate their location. A radio transmitter sends out waves from one location in all directions. A receiver will be loudest when the hiker is facing the transmitter. When the hiker knows the readings from two places, they can find the transmitter.*

In our situation, using an iPad Wi-Fi model, the iPad is the transmitter. The signal is picked up via Apple's database of wireless access points. These access points, either public or private, can be located and mapped. Apple formerly used Skyhook's services and database to fulfill this role, they now have their own and, as you can see if you have location services enabled on your device, their system can be amazingly accurate.

Finding Your Location on the Map

One of the first things people like to do when they open their Maps app is find out exactly where they are on the map. I know, you would think they would know where they are but it's human nature to be curious about some things that are sometimes even quite obvious. I won't go into the psychology of it all (even if I could!) but, all kidding aside, we are sometimes caught, for whatever reason, in a location we are unfamiliar with and need to know. Actually doing this has changed slightly since iOS 6.0. To find out where you are, go to Settings -> Privacy -> Location Services and enable it. Go down to Maps in that column and make sure to enable it, if it's not currently enabled.

Now go to the Maps app and tap the arrowhead icon in the lower left-hand corner of the map. The first time you use the app you will be told that "'Maps' Would Like to Use Your Current Location." You will have two options, "Don't Allow" and "OK." Assuming you still want or need to know where you are, select "OK." The map will close in on your location and the arrow will turn purple. If you move around, the map will continue to update your position. You can zoom in on your location by either double-tapping the screen at the pin spot or pinching out with two or three fingers.

The default map image is what's called the "Standard" image. This is a standard map view looking down on the streets from above. If you tap the curled page in the lower right corner of the screen, there will be additional viewing options. On the newly revealed page, there will also be a "Hybrid" and a "Satellite" option for viewing maps. Most of us are familiar with satellite images now but tap that option and look at the map again. Now the view will include images of the actual landscape around your location. Depending on where you are, you may see an image of the house you're in and a blue dot indicating where, exactly, in the house you're located at the moment. Again, double-tapping or pinching out will provide a closer view. You May be amazed at how accurate the map is.

Now, tap the curling page image again and, this time, select the "Hybrid" option. You are now presented with a map that not only shows your location visually, but also indicates the locations and names of streets surrounding you. Now you know why it's called a "hybrid" map image.

Once again, if you pinch out or double tap you will zoom in on your map and close-up images of your location will come into focus. Apple has been working hard on obtaining fly-over images of many major cities around the world. As of this writing, the number of cities is still somewhat limited but the number may be significantly higher as time goes on. If you're lucky enough to live in, or even visit, one of the included cities, you'll be able to see 3D images of the applicable city, replete with buildings, streets, and cars. You can definitely "Find yourself" on one of these!

Among the list of cities that are currently included among the number of 3D viewable are: Cupertino, CA (Of course! Apple's home base); Sacramento, CA; Los Angeles, CA; San Francisco, CA; Copenhagen, Denmark; Sydney, Australia; Miami, FL; Chicago, IL; Seattle, WA; and, Montreal, Canada. This iOS 6.x feature is absolutely amazing to this baby boomer who remembers getting excited when Radio Shack's TRS-80 computers first came out with color screens! Ah, Nirvana!

Leaving memory lane for a moment, it's possible to view these 3D images by going to the Maps app and entering one of the 3D imaged cities in the search bar on the upper right. A pin will drop at the center of the applicable location. Zooming in, as described above, will bring the desired details. Now, tap 3D in the lower left-hand corner, next to the arrow image, and you'll be struck by the magic that is displayed. Today's technology at its peak. How these renderings are created remains Apple's secret, suffice it to say, the presentation of this work is mind boggling.

Getting to There from Here

Getting Directions

By Automobile

As previously mentioned, the procedure for getting directions has changed somewhat from 5.1.1 to 6.x but to get directions to or from a location, tap the "Search" box in the upper right corner of the app. That should bring the keyboard up. Then either enter a few letters of a contact's name; or tap the open book image to enter a bookmark, recently entered address, or contact from your contact book; or drop a pin by tapping the curling page image, at the bottom right of your screen, and enabling "Drop Pin." From there, go back to the map and tap a spot, once the pin is "Dropped" it can be moved around to different locations by tapping and holding it a couple of seconds then, without lifting your finger or stylus from the screen, slide it to where you'd like it or, at least, in close proximity. You can find out exactly where you dropped it by tapping the little "i," or information icon, on the balloon that comes up when you tap the pin. A final method of getting directions is to enter the zip code and business type (i.e. Pet Shop), or city, state, and business type.

Once your destination pin is on the map, from any of the above methods, either tap the grey "Directions" tab on the top bar or tap the blue circled "i" on the information box that pops up when the pin is tapped and select "Get Directions To" or "From Here" option. If you opt to tap the "i," in the pop up that you'll see there will also be other options. They are: Add to Contacts; Add to Bookmarks; Share Location; and, Report a Problem. Each of these will be discussed in more detail later but, for now, select "Directions to Here." A pop up will then ask where to start from if you've selected the "i" option. Current Location is the default value you will see preselected. If, when you entered your address information or dropped a pin, more than one pin now shows on the map, you will have those additional options listed as potential destinations. Should you realize you wanted the reverse directions, i.e. "Directions From" instead of "To," tap the little up and down squiggly arrow icon to the left of the "Start" - "End" fields.

Once an address is selected in this pop up, select one of the options at the top of this pop up, either the vehicle image for driving directions, the pedestrian image for walking directions, or the bus image for public transportation information. The icon will appear there even if there is no available public transportation for the selected route. Now tap the blue "Route" button to the right of those images. The app will go through some configurations and, if all goes as planned, provide a map image with at least one route. Note, The first time you select "Directions" via either method, you will receive a "Safety Warning," in a green pop up window with white writing. It will ask that you, "Please be safe and always pay attention to the road. Road conditions and directions may change or be inaccurate. Always observe posted road signs and current road conditions." A mouthful of a disclaimer! You will have to tap OK to dismiss the pop up and move on.

Routing information will appear at the top of the screen for the blue flagged route. This information bar across the top will tell you how many routes were found, the time it will take to get there by following the highlighted route, the distance, and the route name, or number, if there is one main route (i.e. 1 of 3). A second bar, which appears under that bar, will inform you of any specific details about the route, such as if tolls are required. A blue "Start" button will be on the right side of the top bar and a grey "Cancel" button on the left.

If there is more than one driving route available, the routes will appear in blue on the map and be numbered from the main route, one, up to the number of routes available with the selected route being a bright blue. Using three as an example, you would see three blue routes each numbered one through three on a little route sign, reminiscent of an old highway route sign. If you tap route two, you will notice that the information on the top bar has changed, now indicating that you are using the second route of three, the driving time required, the distance (in whatever form you've set it for in Settings -> Maps -> Distances, and the main route will again be indicated. The lower bar might have different information as well, depending on the route chosen, such as that the route contains "Restricted Access Roads."

In the lower left hand corner will be an additional tab which is indicated by a lined paper image. If you tap that image, a full listing of directions to the location will appear on the left side of your screen. You can scroll through those listed, turn by turn directions to determine if that is the route you'd like or not. Once you've checked the options for the various routes and made your travel decisions, tap the blue "Start" button on the right side of the top bar. Again, the map will go through a transformation and end appearing as a close-up image of your starting location.

The top bar will now indicate your starting point with a grey "Overview" button on the right and a grey "End" button on the left. Under that bar will be, what appears to be, a green "Road" sign. The road sign will give your first travel instructions for your journey. On the map under it, will be a dot indicating your starting point, with a blue translucent circle surrounding the directions indicated on that road sign I just spoke of. Gone will be the little lined piece of paper in the lower left corner which offered you the option of seeing the full listing of the directions, at least in early versions of iOS 6.x, those will have been replaced with just the road signs.

Now, to see details of your trip, in advance, you'll have to either scroll down on the map and watch as the road signs change as you scroll, or by flicking right to left through the road signs which will, in turn, move your map accordingly. You'll know how many road signs there are by the numbers indicated to the right of your starting point in the top bar. As you move through the signs, the number increases and the total is always shown to give you a sense of accomplishment. I'm sure that's not the reason it's shown but, if you're like me, that's how you'll feel as you move on.

As you travel, your location will be updated on the map, as long as you have an internet connection, but you will have to scroll through the signs one by one as you make the various turns and follow the directions provided on those road signs. Once you've reached your destination, tap the end button on the top bar and thank your iPad.

There are a variety of navigational apps that are available and integrated with the new Maps app since iOS 6.0. They will provide turn by turn spoken directions as well as a variety of other options, I'm sure. Prices vary depending on the features you desire. If developers hold true to form, there will be no shortage of options available to choose from. With iOS 6.0, however, traffic updates are available for many routes. As I mentioned earlier, Siri can be helpful in obtaining directions for you provided you have an iPad third generation or later, a 4G model, and an Internet connection, be it Wi-Fi or 3 or 4G. If all those conditions are met she will provide spoken turn by turn directions in conjunction with the Maps app.

By Walking

To view walking times and directions, tap the pedestrian image I pointed out above when choosing "Get Directions..." before you actually select the route option. After tapping "Route," you will see a similar set up to the one described above with the double grey bars at the top of the page, the three tabs at the bottom (again with the lined list indicating the availability of detailed directions), the grey "Clear" button on the left of the top bar, and the blue "Start" button on the right. Again the map should have at least one mapped out route visible on the screen and the same descriptive elements on those top two bars. To see the detailed directions tap the little lined tab in the lower left and to get the turn by turn directions, tap the blue "Start" button. The rest is exactly the same as for a vehicle.

By Public Transportation

The final method of transportation is public transportation. In iOS 5.x these directions were only provided when public transportation was available between your destination and starting point, as you might conclude. A limit of the Maps app in iOS 6.0 is that you can't get this information without the installation of a third party app. If you select the public transportation option, and tap "Route," a listing of available apps that will provide related information will appear. Also, for example, if you're planning to go to San Francisco, CA for a stay, but live in Buffalo, NY, it is not possible to plan side trips ahead from within the Maps app. This information will only be provided for your destination or origination point; however, there will also be third party, or App Store, programs that will do this sort of thing. As of this writing, this is a limitation of Maps.

That said, to view public transportation routes and information, follow the above steps for setting up your current location and destination, or vice versa, then tap the Bus icon. Select an app to obtain the routing details. There are several free apps listed that are quite good at what they do.

Other Options

To get live traffic information for an area - tap the curling page image and tap "Show Traffic," go back to the map and, if traffic information is available, you'll see colored routes. A green route indicates the speed limit is 50 or over. An amber route indicates the speed limit is 25 to 50 mph. A red route indicates the speed limit is under 25 mph. And, a grey route indicates no traffic information is currently available.

To view street level images, in iOS 5.x, tap the little head in an orange circle. Note, though, the street level photo that appears may be a few years old. Street level views are no longer available in iOS 6.x as they've been replaced with Apple's flyover feature; however, they can be viewed in the Google Maps App or, in Safari, on the Google site.

Finally, at times while creating a route, Maps may say the "Map Server is Not Available." This can be frustrating but the hold up is generally only momentary. You can try again in a few moments and it may then be available.

What Else Will Maps Do for Me

"i" Options

As touched upon earlier, Maps offers more than just mapping routes for you. When you select the "i" option on the pin's bubble, the pop up that comes up offers several options in addition to "Directions From Here" and "Directions To Here." As pointed out, there are four additional options on the bottom of that pop up. In this section, we'll briefly review what each of those options do.

Add to Contacts

The function of the "Add to Contacts" option is fairly self explanatory. When selected, you will decide between "Create New Contact," "Add to Existing Contact," and "Cancel." When "Create New Contact" is selected, a contact form will come up with the address details from the bubble already filled in. If a phone number was also available on the bubble information, that will be entered as well. All that remains is for you to enter the person or place's name.

When the "Add to Existing Contact" option is selected, a list of all your contacts will come up for you to scroll through and select the applicable person, place, or thing to apply information to. In turn, when a contact is then selected, the Map data will be added to that contact. You can then send a message - via the Message app; share the contact information through a social email or, again, Message; or, add the contact information to your bookmarks in Safari. When you're through, your new pin flag will have the applicable information on it referencing your selected contact.

Add to Bookmarks

This option in the information box gives you an opportunity to add the pin info to your Safari bookmarks without applying a contact's name or details to it. When selected, you will have an opportunity to name the bookmark something that will be memorable when you attempt to use it.

Share Location

Share location is a nice little feature of Maps. It allows you to let friends and loved ones know where you are through either, email, the Message app, Twitter, or Facebook. If you change your mind about doing so, you can always tap the "Cancel" button at the bottom of the pop up.

Report a Problem

The final option in the information box is to report a problem. Another option that is self-explanatory and needs no real explanation. When this option is selected, you can report the problem to Apple by indicating the "Information is Incorrect," the "Place does not exist," or "My problem isn't listed." Make your choice then click the blue "Next" button on the upper right. This will take you to another page with a "Comment" box where you can elaborate on the issue and explain it in more detail.

CHAPTER 12

Game Center

Introduction

Signing In

Ｉf you like games, you can hardly go wrong with this app. Actually a collection of apps within an app, Game Center offers a lot of variety for your game choices so, pretty much, no matter what type you enjoy playing, this app has got you covered.

When you first open this app, you'll be asked to enter some identifying information. Don't get too nervous about this, the whole idea behind Game Center is that it allows you to compete in its own virtual social network. You can connect with Facebook friends and compete against them, or you can post your high scores and vie against all other players.

At any rate, submitting your personal information enables you to make these connections. You'll be able to create a user name and choose your privacy level, i.e. who gets to see your name, etc. before you begin. One last point about set up, if you'd like you can add your photo to the app. If you don't choose upon set up, when you open Game Center subsequently, you'll be asked if you'd like Facebook friends who are playing Game Center games to find you. You can Allow this or Deny it, according to how you feel about your privacy.

You can allow Game Center to show you friends' recommendations by enabling this feature in your account settings. You can choose a Public Profile by enabling that as well. What that does is make your real name visible to other players, allow game center to recommend you to other players using your real name, and allow your nickname to be used on public leaderboards.

When you add an email address, it must be verified by Game Center via Apple and it allows people who know your entered email address to send friend requests. A verification link will be emailed to you for each email address you choose to add and you will have to confirm those email addresses in order to use them with Game Center. Your Nickname will be public and will appear in leaderboards and multi-player games.

Getting Around

What's Under the Hood

To play any of the games, just tap their icon on the main page. As far as the games go, only Storm8 Cannon Ball, MetalStorm Wingman,

Robokill 2, Leviathan Five are free. The remainder of Game Center's games need to be purchased to play them.

Looking at that main page, you'll notice that there are several tabs across the bottom, under the lower section of games. The first one will be "Me" (Or whatever you referred to yourself as), next is Friends, Games, Challenges, and, finally, Requests.

Going to the Friends tab will take you to a column on the left with various friend recommendations and a place to add friends. At the top of the column, you'll find you're under the Recent tab in that column. To the left of that tab is A-Z and, to the right, Points. Going to the A-Z tab it mimics the Recent tab unless you've been active recently. Under the Points tab are a listing of various high scores in descending order with the details of the achievements and the Nickname of the high scorer accompanying each score.

At the top of the column, again, all the way to the left is a plus (+) sign. Selecting that brings up a friend request email, with the message pre-filled, just waiting for you to enter an email address. There is also a plus (+) sign to the right of the To field in case you'd like to send an invitation to more than one friend. When done, select Send in the upper right or, if you've changed your mind, Cancel in the upper left.

Going to the next tab across the bottom, you open up the Games section. In this section you'll find a grouping of recommended games from installed games and various other games from your iPad listed below that, in two separate sections. The games will be in their own boxes and indicate the game's; name, whether or not you've ever played it and, if so, when, and the number of rankings for it. At the very bottom of that page will be an option to Find Game Center Games which, when selected, takes you to the App store to find and purchase more Game Center games.

The next tab to the right is Challenges. This page will list the scores your friends have played that you need to beat. You can challenge friends by tapping on the scores or achievements in the game section.

Finally, we have the Requests section. Here you will find a listing of any requests that friends have presented to you to compete against them. If there are none listed, or you just want more, you can tap "Add Friends" which, again, will bring up an email pre-filled and awaiting an email address from you. Send it when you've completed it and you're all set!

Have fun!

CHAPTER 13

Music

Adding Media

The easiest way to add media to your music library is through a computer sync.

To do so:

1. On your computer, open iTunes;

2. Under "Devices" in the left hand column, select your iPad;

3. Once your iPad is selected, go to the "Music" tab on the top of the main window;

4. Select "Sync Music", then you can choose to sync all the music on your computer with your iPad (Note: If you have a large

music library, keep the size of your iPad storage in mind), or you can select to sync playlists, albums, artists, etc.

After making these choices, you can then determine whether or not to sync music videos, voice notes, and/or whether or not to fill space on your iPad with music. I don't recommend this last option as, what little space you have available on your iPad will be taken up with your music not leaving any room for apps, documents, videos, or whatever else you might like to have on it.

Next select the music you'd like to sync and click "Apply" to sync.

Another way to get music on your iPad, if you don't have any or much on your computer or don't have a computer, is to do it right from your iPad. On your iPad go to Settings -> iTunes & App Stores -> Sign In. Enter your Apple user name and password. If you don't yet have one, tap "Create New Account" and follow the instructions to set one up. Then, go to the iTunes app on your iPad, or the "Store" tab from the music app. Make your selections and you'll be all set. Your purchases will download directly to your iPad and back up to iCloud, or your computer if you've set it up that way.

Bringing Up the Controls

There are several ways to bring up the controls for the music app on your iPad. The first one we'll discuss is the most basic of these or what I call the "easy" way. To bring up the controls in the easiest way, from the lock screen, double click the Home button. Your controls will appear at the top of your screen.

Another easy way, when your iPad is unlocked and active, go to the Multitasking Bar by, again, double-tapping the Home button then swipe from left to right. If you're not in an app that has its own audio, your iPod controls will appear.

A not too surprising way of bringing up your iPod or Music controls is from within the Music app itself. When in the Music app, the controls will be at the top of the page.

Familiarizing Yourself With the Controls

Knowing exactly which controls do what may be challenging at first if you're not familiar with the iPod and/or other touch screen MP3 devices. The first control you'll most likely want to be familiar with, even before you play your music, is the volume control. The volume control is in the upper right corner of the app. To turn the volume down, slide the button to the left. To turn the volume up, slide it to the right. Of course, you can always use your volume control buttons on the right side of your iPad, when the home button is at the bottom. Using this button is more visual, and some people prefer to see exactly where that volume adjustment will be when they set it.

The play/pause button is the one with the right facing single arrow if there is no audio playing, or the double vertical lines if audio is playing. It probably goes without saying that, to play your audio, you'll tap that right facing arrow and to pause your audio, tap the double vertical line button, which is the same button with a changed function while activated.

The Previous Track/Rewind button is the button with the double left facing arrows. When a track is playing, tapping this button once will take you to the beginning of the current song. Tapping the very same button twice will take you to the beginning of the previously played song in the playlist, soundtrack, or album. If there is only one song, it will end play and put the app back to start up condition with just the selected playlist window remaining open. Finally, tapping and holding that button will rewind the audio at double speed.

The button to the right of the play/pause button is the Next Track/ Fast Forward button. You would tap it to skip to the next track in the list and tap and hold it to fast forward at double speed.

Finally, we come to what's known as the scrubber bar and play head. The "Scrubber Bar and Play Head" are the names given to the red action line moving along the bar between the time indicators at the center top of the app. The time indicator at the left of it shows the amount of time thats elapsed since the audio started playing and the time indicator on the right of the bar shows how much time is left until the audio is finished playing. The play head is the actual red line that sometimes has a little ball on it. The bar enables you to advance or go back to any portion of the audio track you'd like.

Above this scrubber bar you'll see a sliding indicator with the currently playing song and performing artist. Artist information, soundtrack information, and song indication should alternate into view. On the left of the scrubber bar box will be a picture of the album or soundtrack cover and on the right side of that box will be a white "Genius" symbol, if you are playing a "Genius" song (which we'll discuss further in a few minutes), indicating that it is, in fact, a "Genius" song. The symbol will be uncolored if it's not a Genius song.

Also on the left side of the scrubber bar, between the album art and the time indicator, is a Repeat button. Tap this once to repeat all the tracks in the current list over and over - the button appears black. If you tap it again, the current song will repeat over and over again - the button will appear black with a number one in it. To turn off the repeat function, tap the button again. The button will then turn white.

On the right of the scrub bar, between the time indicator and the Genius symbol, you'll see a shuffle button. If you'd like to mix, or play the audio in a random order, tap this button once. To turn this feature off, tap it again.

While playing a Genius Playlist, if you select the album art work, instead of having a "Store" button and "Search" box on the Bottom of the app, you'll have a back arrow on the left and a list button on the right. The back arrow takes you to the previous page and the album track list button takes you to a list of all the tracks on the currently playing album. Tap any song in the list to play it or you can rate it by swiping across the stars at the top of the column from one for not liking it much to five for liking it very much.

Creating Basic Playlists

There are two types of playlists that can be created on your iPad. The first we'll discuss are what I'll call basic playlists, or playlists created the standard way that you would basically create in iTunes on your computer.

To create a basic playlist, go to the Music app and select "Playlists" in the bottom tab of the app. Click on "New" in the upper right hand corner and name your playlist. An alphabetical listing of all the songs on your iPad will come up. Select the tracks you wish to add to your playlist (Note: You can select from any of the listed songs or from any of the tab selections from the bottom of the app). When you've chosen all the tracks you want included, click "Done" in the upper right corner.

That's it! To play your playlist, select it and a list of all the songs on it will come up. Select one and it will play until you select another or its finished. Then it will go to the next track and continue until it has played the last song in the list, or repeatedly if you've chosen the repeat icon.

Creating Genius Playlists

The next type of playlist we'll discuss is known as the "Genius" playlist. We've discussed playing them when we discussed the controls, now we'll talk about creating them. A Genius playlist is a playlist created by the Music app based on a playing song. The app will create this list based on what it thinks you would like from your music selection. In the Music app, begin playing a song from your song listing. Select the "Genius" icon in the box at the top next to the scrub bar. Now go to the Playlist tab at the bottom of the page and, at the top of the playlist list should be one titled, simply, "Genius Playlist." Select the Genius playlist to see what songs have been included. If you like the playlist that your Music app has created, tap "Save" in the upper right. The playlist will be saved with the title of the first song on the list.

If you don't like the playlist combination, tap "New" to play a different first song or "Refresh" to get a new list of songs. Continue in this fashion until you're satisfied with the list, then save. To play the playlist, select it and tap on a song. It will work as described above in the basic playlist section.

Tabs - Searching for Music and More

The easiest way to find music categorized by playlists, songs, artists, albums, and more, is to use the tabs at the bottom of the app. Tapping on any of those tabs will take you to an alphabetical listing of all music, in the selected category, on your iPad. If you have any tracks in the following categories on your iPad, they will also show in the "More" tab selection. Those categories are: Shared; Genre; Composers; and Audiobooks. In iOS 5.x Podcasts and iTunes U tabs are also here.

Most of you probably know, or at least have some idea of, what shared, genre, composers, and audiobooks would refer to but I think a brief explanation of podcasts and iTunes U are in order here. If you've never heard or seen a podcast, you may not know that they are generally informational talks or videos on a particular subject, usually given by a knowledgeable person in the topic's field. They can, however, also be entertaining as in a comedy podcast. Of course, they all aim to entertain in one way or another, but the type of entertainment varies based on the seriousness of the topic. Podcasts can be attained through the Podcasts app. Podcasts are generally free.

iTunes U, for those of you unfamiliar with it, is a source of many educational courses/workshops/classes, most of which are by instructors and/or professors at well known universities throughout the world. If you enjoy learning new things, I think you're in for a real treat if you search through the many offerings available in iTunes U. These classes, too, can be attained through the iTunes U app. Although both podcasts and iTunes U have been around for quite some time, their apps are relatively new. You can search through the many offerings in both categories either in iTunes on your computer or on your iPad in the respective apps.

Before we leave the More tab, you can additionally use the "Sort By Artist" option to further organize your selections for ease of searching through your tracks.

Audio Settings

Sound Check

It is possible to do what is known as a "Sound Check" on your iPad. What that means basically is that you can adjust the sound on your iPad to even out the volume of one track in relation to another. To do this go to iTunes on your computer and open Preferences in "iTunes", on a Mac, or in "Edit" on a PC. Click the playback tab then enable "Sound Check" by checking that box.

Now, on your iPad, go to Settings - > Music, and turn "Sound Check" on. That's it! There should be a balance now in the volume of your tracks from one to another.

Volume Settings

You can also set the audio level on Your iPad to a maximum volume so you don't have to suffer from a suddenly blaring track. To do so, go to Settings -> Music -> Volume Limit on Your iPad and adjust the setting to a maximum that you would enjoy if the volume was all the way up. Once done, if you'd like you can passcode lock the setting by selecting "Volume Limit" in Settings -> General -> Restrictions -> Allow Changes on your iPad.

Once you've set the volume slider in the Music settings, you'll be all set with music and videos on any connected speaker. However, that setting doesn't affect the volume of audiobooks, iTunes U, or any sound coming from the iPad's built-in speaker.

Equalizer Settings

If you like more or less bass or other frequencies, you can also adjust the equalizer settings on your iPad to your taste. If the quality of the audio doesn't meet your standards, on your iPad go to Settings -> Music -> Equalizer. The best thing to do is to play a song in the background and adjust accordingly.

Note: Using the iPad with the equalizer on uses more battery so, unless you play audio regularly, you may prefer to only change these settings when you do and keep them off in between.

Audiobooks, Podcasts, iTunes U

You can access audiobooks, through the Music app. Go to the "More" tab on the bottom of the page and select the applicable category. A page will open with all of the existing folders containing your audio tracks in the selected category, to play one, tap a folder and a list of the included tracks will appear. Select the track you would like to play by tapping it, adjust the volume accordingly, and that's all there is to it!

Just a note about Podcasts and iTunes U. I recommend the content of both of these offerings be reviewed, as I'm sure you'll find something of interest in one and/or the other and all is free; however, content for and listening to these two great features is from within these respective apps themselves since iOS 5.1.1.

```
┌─────────── CHAPTER 14 ───────────┐
│                                  │
│                                  │
│              iTunes              │
│                                  │
└──────────────────────────────────┘
```

Overview

iTunes

Almost simultaneously released were iOS 6.0 and a totally revamped iTunes. If you're at all familiar with iTunes on a PC or Mac, this app will be very familiar to you. It doesn't stray much from those versions in usage. The big difference between the two is the absence of the App Store within it but, as we'll discuss, that store has its own app on the iPad.

So let's take a look around. When you enter the store for the first time, you'll be taken to the Music section of the iTunes store. If, by chance you've been in the app before, you'll be taken to the last section you were in when you left the iTunes app.

No matter which of the first four sections you're taken to, the overall appearance will be the same with the only change being to the content. We will discuss the sections specifically in a few minutes but, in general, across the top of the app in those first four sections are four categories which vary based on the section you're in. For example, in the TV Shows section the four tabs are: All Genres, Animation, Classic, and More. We'll discuss the specific sections individually in the following pages but, before we do, there are three more sectional tabs across the bottom: Charts; Genius; and Purchased. While downloading any of your purchases, you'll have an additional "Downloads" section. Returning to the top of the screen in the Music, Movies, TV Shows, and Audiobooks sections, you will see that, to the right of the aforementioned category tabs is a series of short horizontal lines, resembling a sheet of lined paper, which represents, in Apple talk, a list. When tapped it elicits a drop-down menu with your history and, to the right of that list icon is a search box. Of course, if you know what you're looking for, the easiest thing to do is conduct a search for it. In most cases, though, people just like to browse and see what's new or being featured, and that's where the other tabs come in.

Across the bottom of all pages, regardless of section, you'll find seven tabs representing the sections we've been referring to. The tabs are: Music, Movies, TV Shows, Audiobooks, and, as stated above, Charts, Genius, and Purchased. Now let's look at each section individually.

Music

Getting the Ho Down

We'll begin this iTunes app by discussing the Music section, after all, iTunes, other than for apps, is probably best known for its music selections. Viewing the Music section page the category tabs across the tab will be: All Genres, Tones, Alternative, and More.

All Genres is, of course, the all inclusive category. Each of the other category listings across the top are covered under this tab. To be more selective with your shopping, you may decide you'd like to go right to the specific genre rather than sifting through everything to get to what you eventually want. To do this, you can find a variety of music genres under tones as well as dialogue and sound effects.

Choosing Alternative you will find a variety of new and many unknown artists and recordings. Always fun to explore and sometimes pleasant surprises will be found here. The last category tab, More, is Music again. It's beyond my understanding why Apple has decided to list "All Genres" under Music in the More category in addition to the obvious "All Genre" category tab to the far left, but maybe my readers can enlighten me here. On the surface, I see no difference but I don't do a lot of Music shopping in iTunes I'm sorry to say. For those of you who do, I'm sure you'll be able to explain this to me easily because, I'm sure, Apple has to have a reason for this redundancy.

At the bottom of the rows of listings are two boxes the first of which contains your Apple ID and the next is a Redeem option. You can tap "Redeem" to use gift cards or download codes if you have any.

Except for the main Music page, many of the other pages you might select are laid out pretty similarly. At the top will be something similar to "New and Noteworthy," followed by Albums, Singles, and Top Songs, not necessarily in that order. The main page is of course much more showy with a slider screen at the top displaying featured music but most of the remainder are fairly standard in layout.

Movies

Cinematography

Moving on to the Movies section, the main page there is laid out like the main Music sections page. You'll see the slider at the top showing featured films, followed by New and Noteworthy, The Movie of the Week and similarly categorized films, Great Documentaries, and Great Franchises. These will be followed by two boxes the first of which contains your Apple ID and the next is that Redeem option, again. As explained earlier, you can tap "Redeem" to use gift cards or download codes if you have any.

To more closely examine a particular movie, tap it and you'll see a plot summary, possibly a trailer, the ratings by other shoppers who have purchased it, and the pricing information. To buy or rent it, tap the applicable button on the detail page. Before you buy, you can choose, in most cases, between an HD and an SD version, by tapping the button of your choice on the far right of the "Rent" or "Buy" buttons on that same page. When you tap the HD version option, you'll notice a price difference. The HD or High Definition option, is generally a clearer, more defined image - thus the name high definition - so comes with a higher price tag. The SD or Standard Definition version will, naturally, be a little cheaper for both renting and buying.

If you scroll down that detail page, you'll see the Cast and Crew listings as well as language and copyright information. There are generally three tabs to access the sections mentioned above, i.e. Details, Ratings and Reviews, and Related. I've mentioned the Details and Ratings and Reviews already but the Related, when selected, will show you other movies that have been purchased by other shoppers at the same time. Some may be very similar in theme to the one you're viewing at the moment and that is usually the case, but there are times when the movies mentioned in this section seem totally "unrelated."

A last point on the detailed listings is that there is a share option. If you tap the little action icon (the button with a right facing arrow coming out of a box), in the upper right corner of the detail box, you'll find you can mail, tweet, post to Facebook, or copy the link to this listing. Facebook is new in iOS 6.x as, with this iteration of the operating system, it became fully integrated into the system. When any of the options mentioned are chosen, you will be presented with the applicable window to complete the action. When the "Copy Link" option is chosen, you won't "see" anything, but you will now be able to paste that link into a message, an email, a note to yourself, or anyplace else you may choose to.

When you've finished looking at the detail page you can do one of three things. You can tap outside the box and you will be taken back to the row that the movie you were viewing was listed in on the main Movie page, which you can then scroll through. You can tap "See All" in the upper right corner of the page, in which case you'll be taken to a two column listing of Top Movies. Or, finally, you can tap "Done" in the upper left corner of the page in which case you'll be brought back to the opening or main page of the Movie section.

Looking across the top of the main page, you'll notice that it, too, is broken down into the four category set up that the Music section was but these categories are: All Genres, Action and Adventure, Classics, and More. To the right of these will be the same list - which takes you to your previous shopping history and, to the right of that, the same search box.

An exploration of these various tabs will show a similar breakdown to that of the Music section right down to the More category which, like the Music section, includes All Genres, and the categories included in the All Genres category tab. Again, I can't explain the redundancy upon closer inspection you may find some differences, but this will come with a more detailed search.

When one of these tabs is selected, the visible page will resemble the main page but may be missing the top slider. It, too, will be broken down into three or four scrollable rows. The row headings vary, based on the category you choose, but following that heading, you'll notice a "See All" option with a little right facing arrow to the right of it. To view all "New and Noteworthy" for example, tap that little "See All" arrow and you'll be directly taken to a page of all "New and Noteworthy" movies. To return to the previous page from any of these sections, just tap the "Back" button in the upper left corner and you'll be taken back to the previous page.

That's about it for Movies, now on to the TV Shows section…

TV Shows

Main Page

Arriving at the Main page of the TV Shows section you pretty much see more of the same. The layout in this section is almost identical to the Music section. The top row is Hit TV Shows, followed by a row of some categorized shows (Such as by network), then New and Noteworthy, before the Latest TV Episodes. As in Movies and Music, the top row is a slider of featured TV Shows.

If this is your first time in this section, you will be taken to the All Genres tab at the top. The other three tabs are: Animation, Classic, and More. And, once again, you have your History drop down and Search box.

The Animation and Classic pages give a little bit different look, but the breakdowns are consistent with other sections and categories. The More tab differs from the All Genres for a change. At the top of the More category is All Genres, which is exactly the same as the first tab's All Genres. Under More, however, the various categories are more specific. The listing includes such shows as: Comedy, Drama, Kids, etc.

Selecting one of the specific categories will take you to page listing Latest TV Episodes, followed by New and Noteworthy, Top TV Episodes, and Top TV Seasons. There are two sections of listings and two scrollable rows of larger images in each section.

This basically covers the TV Show section. Again, if you know what you're looking for, the easiest way to find it is to enter a keyword in the search box and conduct a search for it. If not, try to eliminate as many variables as possible by going to the specific category and, if possible, section, that would apply.

Audiobooks

Listening to a Good Book by the Fireplace

A separate Audiobooks tab in iTunes is a new feature in iOS 6.0. The page layout is more of the same. It's basically identical to the first three sections in appearance, only the content differs. Again there are four rows of scrollable titles. To get to the bargains, you have to scroll down to the bottom of the page. The final column is "Great Audiobooks $5.95 or Less." Now in my book, that's a bargain that's hard to pass up! Then again, there are few bargains I can pass up, again, much to my husband's chagrin.

Charts

Keeping Up With the Joneses

I mention elsewhere in this book that, if you like keeping up with the Joneses, this is the place for you. Well here is another place for you. Listed here are the tops in each of several categories. Generally, these are the top grossing in their respective genres and categories. The three genres are Music, Movies, and TV.

Within Music you'll find the top Music Videos and Albums. Within Movies, the top grossing Movies, and, within TV the top TV Seasons and top TV Episodes. Again, not to make light of these lists, they help many shoppers who are confused about what might be a worthwhile download and, seeing ratings by others who have already viewed and/or listened to the media helps them narrow down their selections, especially with such a wide variety being offered. This is nothing to be ashamed of and, I have to admit, I frequently read and am influenced by reviews. Not always, but sometimes. Feel free to use these ratings to your advantage; that's why they're there.

Genius

Let's See What You Might Like

Genius is a carryover from the Music app and was new in iOS 6.0 for iTunes on the iPad. What this feature is all about is predicting, based on your past selections, what you might like to purchase in the future. Pretty "ingenious" of Apple (No pun intended, OK so it was!). Who would have thought years ago that this type of sales technique would be built into computer software?! I know I never would have, then again there's a lot of technology it would have been hard to imagine when home computers first made the scene.

Basically, that's all there is to Genius. If you have never made a purchase or downloaded music or videos of some sort, Genius will be unable to make a prediction and will therefore present a blank page in those categories. I can tell you from my personal iPad selections that the Music category is subdivided into Albums and Songs, but, having no Movie or TV purchases to speak of, I can't say what the other two categories look like. You'll have to enlighten me by email or on my site at http://GrandmaTalksTech.com.

Purchased

Now What Did I Buy?!

When you get to this section, if you're at all like me, you'll be wondering what in the world you've bought now. Well, all of your questions will be answered in an orderly fashion by going to the applicable category: Music, Movies, and TV Shows. If that weren't enough, it will be broken down further by everything in iTunes on the computer you sync with, and what's not on your iPad from that list.

If you go to TV Shows, for example, and select any of the purchases you've made via iTunes (again that includes free titles), that title will appear on the right side of your screen in a second column. A cover shot thumbnail image will be to the left of that listing; then the title of the show with the source under it; and, all the way to the right in the listing will be a cloud icon with a down arrow in it. This is indicating that it is currently in the cloud but can be downloaded to your iPad by tapping that icon.

If you elect to download that title to your iPad, a new tab will appear on the bottom by the name of Downloads. A badge will appear on top of the tab indicating how many titles are currently downloading. As the downloads complete, the number will decrease until no number badge remains at which point the Downloads icon will disappear as well. While selecting titles to download, the best thing to do is go to the Not On This iPad tab at the top and make your selections from there, to be sure you're not downloading a title more than once - especially with space at a premium.

Speaking of space, don't forget that movie and TV show files take a lot of free space with generally very large file sizes. In this case, you may want to restrict the number of each that you keep on your iPad at any one time and, as you view them, delete them from your device. Don't delete them from iTunes, only your device. An easy way to do this is, when you're syncing with your computer - in iOS 5.1.1 the sole means for getting these files onto your iPad - deselect the movie or show in question and sync again. This will remove it from your iPad only.

Realize that the only purchased titles in any category will be iTunes purchases, even if you've purchased your media elsewhere. Also note, it is possible to download all songs from the same artist by selecting the cloud on the top line in the right hand column.

Downloads

If you go to the Downloads tab while Music choices are downloading, you'll see the cover image, the title and source, the size of the file downloaded already, the total file size, and approximately how much time remains to complete the download. All items that are downloading will be shown in their own box in a two column format.

In the upper right corner of the Downloads page will be a Purchased button. When that is selected you will be taken to a Playlist titled Purchased. You'll be within the Music app at that point and can play your downloaded music from there.

After your downloads are complete, as I said, that tab will disappear from the bottom of the page. If you were downloading a movie or TV show, all that will remain is a search bar at the top left of that column. To actually view either a movie or TV show, you'll need to go to the Video app.

One final point on the matter of downloading movie or any video file, if you're uncertain as to whether or not the movie you're considering is the one you really want to see, you can view a trailer by selecting the video in question in the right column. There you will also see a description of the video, a rating, and a release date. On that preview page, you'll also be able to share that clip via email, Twitter, or Facebook. An additional option will be to copy and paste the link anywhere you choose. One reason for doing so may be that, at a later time you want to watch it but don't currently have the luxury of time. In such a case you may wish to paste the link in a note to yourself so you don't have to later repeat the search process.

That wraps up iTunes!

CHAPTER 15

Newsstand

New in iOS 5.0, and pretty much unchanged in 6.0, is the Newsstand app. This is where all your iTunes store subscriptions are kept. In its latest form, subscriptions can be purchased from within the app itself by selecting the "Store" button.

Upon entering the Store, you'll see three rows of magazine listings broken down into: New and Noteworthy, What's Hot, and, All Newsstand Apps with a feature magazine slider at the top of the page. Flicking through these categories will take you to even more offerings.

Closer inspection will show "Newsstand" listed at the upper left with four other categories across the top of the window: All Categories, Books, Business, and More. Across the bottom of the screen will be the five classifications: Featured, Charts, Genius, Purchased, and Updates. If you've taken a peek at the App store yet, these will be familiar - the reason being, the Newsstand Store is a subsection of the App Store.

Selecting any of the other options across the top or the bottom will take you out of the magazine subscription section.

Under the third row of the magazine listings should be a box with your Apple ID and a "Redeem" box. Selecting Redeem will open up a small window in which you can list your gift card or coupon code, should you have one. Many of the listed magazines will indicate that they're free and, if you select them, in many cases, you'll find that the first issue is indeed free with subsequent issues costing various amounts.

To leave the store and go back to your subscriptions, tap the "Newsstand" button on the upper left of the window. There you will, again, see any subscriptions that you have "purchased." When I say purchased, it includes any free or gifted subscriptions you may have selected as well. Two points worth mentioning are:

1. If you tap any of the other tabs across the bottom, you'll be taken to the app store and totally out of the Newsstand app with the only way back in being to again tap the newsstand icon from the multitasking or home screen.

2. If you tap the tabs across the top, you'll see a large selection, however, not all are reading material. Many are apps most of which have some peripheral relation to reading. So make sure you know what you are buying before you actually buy it. Note, the tabs at the top all contain a link back to the Newsstand app, so you won't get lost.

CHAPTER 16

Calendar

Looking Around

Keeping Up With Time

All right, so I just liked the title. Don't think you're going to get any pearls of wisdom in the time management department here! What we will talk about here is using the Calendar app to its fullest. This app, similar to the Notes and Mail apps, is a basic, no frills app that will get the job done, even if not handsomely.

On the surface, any changes in the app from iOS 5.1.1 to 6.0 appear to be minimal. One thing worth noting, if you've never noticed, is that the Calendar icon itself is dynamic not static. It changes each day and indicates the correct day and date on it. If you're ever unsure of either, all you have to do is look at your home page and, at a glance, you'll see exactly what day it is.

As far as creativity goes, that's about it with this app. Let's examine it more closely…

Let's Have a Look-See

Usually, upon opening this app, it'll be on the current day's page. Your appointments will be listed down the left column in a sort of bulleted list. The day and date will be at the top of that column. On the right side of the page a monthly calendar with the current date highlighted in blue will be at the top. Below that, in the same column, the day will be broken down into the numbered hour and unnumbered half hour time slots. The day will start at the portion of the time which displays the current time and any appointments you may have in that time period will be indicated in a blue box.

Across the very top of the page in a brown leather appearance, like an old time calendar, there will be several divisions. On the far left is a Calendars button. Selecting this button will elicit a drop-down with a listing of all of your existing and synced calendars. If you have calendar invites, to the right of that, will be a box with a down facing arrow and a number in parentheses. Tapping that button will bring up the word "Invitations" if invitations are outstanding, and "No Invitations" if none are outstanding. I don't think all of the kinks have been worked out of this feature as of this writing because, although invitations were sent, received, and accepted, the number in parentheses never changed. The calendar indicated the invitation was accepted, and by whom, but that was the extent of it. I've got to believe that this button will eventually indicate the number of outstanding invitations but, only time will tell.

To the right of the "Invitations" box is a series of buttons indicating: Day, Week, Month, Year, and List. Selecting any of these will take you to the respective pages. List takes you to a listing of all of your scheduled events with the next one on the right side of the page. The list on the left is scrollable. It begins with the current day's date but will change as you scroll back or forward to other days, months, etc.

Finally, to the right of the boxes listed above, is a Search box which, if you enter an event title or keyword, will take you directly to the applicable event. Moving to the bottom of the page, on the far left is a button that says "Today." Tapping that will take you directly to the current day's entries. To the right of that are a series of dates. If you're in the Day mode, it will be individual dates which go as high as the current month that you're in. On the right of that is an abbreviation for the next month and on the left an abbreviation for the prior month. On either side of those listed dates are a left facing and a right facing arrow, respectively. If you're in the week mode, those numbers will indicate a one week date range, monthly will be a listing of the months, year mode will have a listing of years - going at least as high as 2050, after which I got tired of looking. List mode will take you back to a listing of the current month and the dates in it.

Last but not least, on the very right of the numbers at the bottom of the page, is a plus (+) sign. Tapping that plus sign will cause a pop up to appear which will enable you to add an event. As that plus (+) sign is on the very bottom of the page, it will appear on each and every day and/or date that you choose, enabling you to add an event from wherever you happen to be within the app.

Adding an Event

As I said, we're going to tap that plus (+) sign to enter a new event. When the pop up window comes up, the cursor will be on the top line in the "Title" position. Just fill in the name of the event you would like to schedule, the location goes on the next line.

Under the location there is a date and time section. It will be pre-filled with the date and time that you had selected before tapping the plus sign. To change it, tap the date/time entry. A "Start & End" window will slide into view. Like an old bicycle lock, set the date and time for the start information. The end time should fill in automatically for an hour later or whenever you've set your default appointment allotment for. If you'd rather make it an "All-day" event instead, just move the slider to the "On" position. Don't forget to set the time zone for the event so that your reminders are scheduled appropriately. When you're finished, tap Done. If you change your mind before doing so, you can always Cancel out of it by selecting that option on the upper left.

After you tap Done you'll be brought back to the "Add Event" box. You can now choose if you want your event to repeat and, if so, how often. Options are: None, Every Day, Every Week, Every 2 Weeks, Every Month, and Every Year. If it's a birthday, for example, you'll want to schedule it for every year and set your reminders accordingly. Again, select Done or Cancel when you're through.

Back on the Add Event screen again, you can choose to invite others from your contact list to the event. They'll be sent an invitation to your event on which they can either accept, deny, or say maybe. You'll automatically be notified of their response.

Don't forget to set your alerts. These little alarms can be set for your choice of nine different times, however, custom is not one of them. Don't forget to set it when you're through by selecting Done. Next select the calendar you'd like to schedule this event on. You can also choose how to show your availability during this appointment time.

If there is a URL associated with this event, you can add that here as well as make any applicable notes. When all the necessary information is entered, again select Done. Don't forget, you can always cancel out of an event any time before you tap Done, after that, the event would have to be deleted to clear it from your calendar.

A Final Glance

One final look back will show that a weekly view, as well as a daily view, will be broken down into time slots with your appointments color coded to correspond with your various calendars. The monthly view will not be broken down into hours but will be color coded like the weekly and daily views. The yearly view, too, will be color coded but differently from the other views. Birthdays and appointments will be indicated. And the current month calendar and date will be blue.

Also, if you're connected via Facebook, birthdays will already be filled in, so if you enter them as well, you'll have duplicate entries for each of those. That pretty much wraps up the Calendar app. We'll discuss a few other nice calendar apps available in the app store when we get to Chapter 28.

CHAPTER 17

Reminders

There have been no noticeable changes in the Reminders app from 5.1.1 to 6.0. There is, however, a difference in the app between iPad Wi-Fi models and 3G and 4G models. The main difference being, on the 3 and 4G models with an active wireless connection, reminders can be set based on location as well as time.

Again, you must enable location services for the app in Settings -> Privacy -> Location Services and turn Location Services "On." You can then tap the right facing arrow to the right of "Reminders" and, if so desired, enable these services for any related apps that may request your location to function at their capacity. Keep in mind, not all apps that request use of your location will actually need it and the more apps that use those services, the greater the battery drain.

From those settings, go down to "Reminders" in the main Settings and choose the length of time you'd like to include in your syncing of this app. Options are: Reminders 2 weeks back, ...1 month back, ...3 months back, ...6 months back, and, All Reminders. Once this is set, you can choose the default reminder list you would like to sync with, if you have more than one. Now you're all set to begin using Reminders.

3G and 4G Models With Active Wireless Connections

If you own a 3G or 4G model with and active wireless connection, you can set reminders to let you know, or do, something when you arrive or depart a particular location. For this feature to work properly, you must have the address of the location in question in your contacts list. There are several ways of getting that information into your device, the most obvious of which is to look it up in the phone book and hand enter it into your Contacts app.

Additionally, while at the location on any prior occasion, you can have your iPad get your location and save it in your Contact list with the name of the location (see Chapter 11 on Maps). Finally, you can look online in YellowPages.com, or using their mobile app, and save it to your contacts.

To set a reminder for arriving or departing a location, open your Reminders app by tapping it. On the left side of your screen will be your reminder list categories.

It will be broken down as follows:

◆ Completed - when selected, this category will show a listing of all your completed reminders,

◆ Today - when selected, this category will show a list of all reminders scheduled for the current date,

◆ Reminders - when selected, this will show a list of all reminders in this category on the right side, and

◆ Create New List... - when selected, your cursor will appear where those words were and your keyboard will pop up for you to add a new reminder category with whatever name you enter at this point.

Once you enter the name of this new category, that name will also appear in that left column with "Create New List..." under it. Nothing will appear on the right when the new category is selected until you add reminders to it.

At the top of the left column will be an "Edit" button with a search box under it. To find a particular reminder by name, date, or keyword, enter your search criteria in the field next to the magnifying glass then tap "Return" on your keyboard or the magnifying glass on your screen. A list of all applicable reminders will come up listed under the search box. Select the one you want and see it, in full, on the right. A "Cancel" button will have appeared at the top of the left column. When you're through, you can either search for another reminder by tapping the circled "x" to the right of the search field and entering new criteria, or tap the "Cancel" button at the top of the left column and returning to the Category listing.

Selecting the "Edit" button at the top of that left column will present you with a white dash in a red circle to the left of your added categories, that is, those listed under the translucent white divider between "Today" and "Reminders." Tapping any of these dashes will delete the particular category it's to the left of. A red button with the word "Delete" in white writing will come up on the right of the category name, selecting that

"Delete" button will initiate a delete confirmation pop up. If you're sure you want to delete the category, tap "Delete," If you've changed your mind or are uncertain, you can select the "Cancel" button and nothing will happen. The red Delete button will no longer appear to the right of the category name but the white dashes will remain. If you've decided to leave everything as is, tap the "Done" button at the top. If you've gone ahead and deleted a category, the category will no longer be there and the white dashes will also be gone. At that point you can also tap the white Done button at the top.

Finally, at the bottom of that left column will be a monthly calendar reflecting the current month. The date will be highlighted in bright white numerals on the calendar. You can change the month to an earlier month by tapping the left facing arrow to the left of the month name on the calendar, and to a future month by tapping the right facing arrow on the right.

Setting Up a Reminder

To set up a location based reminder, select Today, Reminders, or another category from the list on the left. You cannot set a reminder from the "Completed" category. That category can only be edited for deletions. Deletions in that category are handled in the same fashion that category deletions are handled.

Once in your chosen category, tap the plus (+) sign at the upper right of the right hand column. A checkbox will appear on the next line on the right, your cursor will appear to the right of the checkbox, and your keyboard will pop up. Enter your reminder information, i.e. what you want to be reminded of. When finished, tap the "Return" key on the keyboard and the cursor and a new checkbox will appear in the next line, ready for your next reminder.

Tap the line you just entered and a "Detail" box will pop up. Your reminder text will be on the first line. The second line will say "Remind Me" and, by default, "Never" will be to the right of those words with a right facing arrow to the right of that. When you tap that arrow a "Remind Me" window will open. On the first line it will say "On a Day" and the next line will say "At a Location." On the right of each of those options will be an On/Off slider at the default setting of "Off." To be reminded based on a location, slide the second slider to the right, enabling it.

When this is done three more lines will drop down. The first line will say Current Location and provide the address. To the right of that line will be an arrow. Tap the arrow to change the location. A Location page will appear. The first line will, again, indicate "Current Location" with the applicable address. The next line will say "Home" with that address listed. This may or may not be the same as the current location, depending on where you are when you schedule the reminder. The last line will be a "Choose Address" option. To select an address other than those listed on the first two lines, select this option. Your contact list will appear with the last location you selected in this app visible. You can choose something in contact "Groups" by selecting that option, you can scroll through your contacts to select one of them, or, if you've changed your mind, you can cancel out of everything and go back to the previous "Location" screen. You must select a contact with an address entered as indicated earlier. After making your selection, you will be returned to the "Location" screen with the "Choose Address" screen completed and a check mark after it. If you're all set with that location, tap the "Remind Me" button on the upper left to return to the prior

"Remind Me" screen. Next, select either the "When I Leave" or "When I Arrive" option. A check mark will appear next to your choice to indicate your selection.

You can then also choose a day that you want to be reminded if, for example, you go to or leave the selected location every day. If you enable that option a new line with a date and time will appear. Tapping on that line will bring up a date and time stamp. Adjust these settings accordingly, then tap "Done" or "Cancel." Either choice will take you back to the "Details" page where, again, "Done" and "Cancel" will be options along with "Delete." Should you choose "Cancel" you'll be taken back to the "Reminders" list and all data previously entered regarding date and/or location will be gone when you return to that page.

Selecting "Done," on the other hand, brings all reminder information forward to your reminders list. Before making your final decision, you may find you want to add more detail,. To do so, select the "Show More" option. You will then have the additional options of setting the priority of the reminder, choosing the list it will appear on (again, if you have more than one list), and writing any notes regarding the reminder that you would like to keep with it.

Finally, selecting the "Delete" option erases the reminder in its entirety from your list. If you've added a date and time to your reminder, you will have the added option of if and when to have that reminder repeated. Options are: None - if you don't want any further reminders, Every Day, Every Week, Every 2 Weeks, Every Month, and Every Year. Confirming your selections by tapping "Done" will bring you to your list where it will remain until acted upon at which time you can check the checkbox putting the reminder in your "Completed" list for future reference or deletion (whichever you choose).

Wi-Fi Models

Setting up reminders on Wi-Fi models is basically the same procedurally, but you won't have the location option. The reminders can only be time based. Location based reminders function primarily with the GPS abilities of your iPad and, as indicated in Chapter 11 on Maps, the Wi-Fi model does not have that functionality but, instead, works on triangulation which, again, is explained in greater detail in that same chapter.

CHAPTER 18

The Clock App

The Clock Application

Clocks

New in iOS 6.0, replacing YouTube, is the Clock app. Opening this app for the first time will bring you to World Clocks. If, by chance, you've been here before, it will bring you to the last section you were in when you left it.

World Clocks

In World Clocks, you'll see six clock faces across the top half of the screen. The first two Cupertino, CA, and New York, NY are white or black, depending on what time of day it is when being viewed. The other four Paris, Beijing, Tokyo, and a blank one with a plus (+) sign in the middle for you to add any other clock you may choose from the listed clocks that will appear when you tap the plus sign. Should you decide you don't need one of the clocks that are currently showing but would like a different one, select the Edit button on the upper left of the screen and a pop up window will list all the existing clocks with a white minus (-) sign in a red circle to the left of each. To delete the one you no longer want, tap the minus sign and a red delete button will appear on the right side of the city's name. Just tap the delete button to eliminate the selected clock. If you tap the wrong minus sign, or change your mind, just tap the minus sign again and no harm done. You can also tap Edit again or anywhere outside that window and you'll be taken back to the clock screen. If you accidentally delete one or later decide you really would like to have that clock, you'll be able to put it back, so don't get flustered. There's very little you can do that can't be undone easily enough or, sometimes, with a little effort.

When you've filled up the six clocks on the top part of the screen, you can scroll to the right to find six more if you need or want them. As you fill six clocks, six more will appear on a new screen that you'll be able to scroll to. You will notice that, depending on time of day, world clocks will either be black or white.

At any rate, to add clocks just tap the little plus sign in their center. To get more detail about one of the cities whose clock is displayed, tap the clock. The image will zoom in, taking up most of your screen real estate, and the current temperature of that location will be illustrated in the upper right. The city name, day and date will be indicated in the center above the clock. An arrow saying "World Clock" will be in the upper left. Tapping this arrow will return you to the previous screen. If you'll notice, under the clock there will be a number of dots, usually at least six and one of the dots will be white while the others are a dark grey. As is the case with most screens on your iPad, this indicates that there are six screens the white one indicates which screen you are currently on. So, if you scroll to the left or the right, depending on what page you are currently on, you will be able to see other screens. In this case, scrolling takes you to the details of your other specified clocks. Note as you go that the white dot has now moved with you and you'll clearly see how many pages are to the right and to the left of the one you are on. If you've added more than six clocks, there will be as many dots as the number of clocks you've set up.

Moving to the lower half of your screen, you will see a map of all the areas covered by the clocks with the digital time, place, and temperature indicated for each of the clocks selected at the top. At the top of the map you'll see the dots representing the number of pages or screens you have on the upper half of your screen. That covers World Clocks. Now we'll move on to Alarms.

Alarms

Tapping the Alarm tab at the bottom of the screen for the first time will bring you to pretty much a blank page. At the top will be a black box split in quarters with an on/off switch to the right of it. Under that will be the days of the week listed horizontally across the screen and, under that, will be a large black box divided into a number of boxes in columns under the respective days. In the center of that box it will say "No Alarms." At the very top of the page will be the word "Edit" to the left, "Alarm" in the center, and a plus (+) sign to the top right.

To set an alarm, tap the plus sign in the upper right corner. An "Add Alarm" drop down box will appear. At the bottom of the box will be clock settings with the current time selected. Change these settings to the desired time. At the top of the box, you can set the alarm to repeat never, or on a particular day of the week. You can also choose to have the alarm repeat every day by selecting all the days of the week. The next option is the sound. By default, it will be Marimba, but you can change this by tapping the right facing arrow to the right of it. There you'll be able to "Buy More Tones," pick a song from your iPad music, or select another ringtone from your iPad's existing ringtones. When you're done, tap the Back arrow which will return you to the setting window. Next you can choose whether to snooze or not, and, finally, you can give this setting a name. If you're not fussy, you can decide to leave it called "Alarm" but, you may want to be alerted for a reason and decide to call the alarm whatever the reason is. Or maybe even Henry or Sue, I don't know. At any rate, just tap the right facing arrow next to "Label" and the keyboard will pop up. You can delete "Alarm" and go ahead and enter the name of your choosing.

Once set, tap "Save" in the upper right to save your settings. If you've changed your mind, as in most situations, you'll have the "Cancel" option. Your alarm should be set to go at your desired time once you've saved it, and it should be indicated on the screen which now shows time slots along the left side of the big black box. Don't worry if you've inadvertently set your alarm for the wrong day or the wrong time. This, too, can be fixed. Just go to "Edit" at the top of your screen, tap the white minus sign in the red circle, then tap the delete button. If you find you want the alarm but wanted it somehow different than what you had set, tap the arrow to the right of the time indicated, and you'll once again have an opportunity to fine tune it. Make the appropriate changes, save, and tap either edit or anywhere outside that window to exit the alarm settings. You should now see the alarm set at the correct time and day slots on the schedule. Once you've saved the settings the alarm should be "On" with the time of the alarm indicated on the clock that now shows at the top of the screen in the formerly empty black box. If, for whatever reason, you are unable to determine the time of one of your alarm settings, the easy way to check it is to just select it on the schedule and the time will show on the clock.

Finally, if for example, you set an alarm for every day at 5am and decide one day you want to sleep until you wake up naturally, just turn the alarm off for that day by editing the days of the week that you want it on for. Don't forget to go back in and reset it for the next time, but enjoy that morning of ease first.

Stopwatch

The next tab brings us to one large stopwatch! Its workings are fairly self-explanatory if you've ever used a stopwatch. If you haven't, to begin timing an event, tap the "Start" button. The timer will begin counting and the "Start" button will become a "Lap" button. If someone is running or walking laps, tap this button each time they complete one and the watch will count the laps and indicate the time taken for that lap as well as the overall time.

When the "Start" button has been activated, the "Reset" button becomes a "Stop" button. That stop button actually functions like a

"Pause" button. It stops the clock but not totally. If you again press "Start," counting will pick up from where it left off, as long as you haven't reset it. When done timing, just tap "Reset" and you're ready to begin again from scratch.

Timer

Next is the "Timer." The timer does just the opposite of the stopwatch. The stopwatch adds up the time until the end, the Timer counts down the time until the end. When this tab is selected, there will be a timer in the middle of the screen with 15 minutes indicated on it, the first time you open it. Set the timer for the amount of time you want to pass before being notified of the ending time. When you're ready to begin, tap the Start button. That button becomes a "Done" button. There is also a "Pause" button should you decide to stop everything for a second. At the end of the specified period of time, there will be a sound. The default is crickets, but you can change this if you'd like by tapping "Sounds" on the upper left side of your screen and selecting another sound. Again, you'll have the option to buy more sounds, and you'll also have the option to stop playing sounds. The sound you've chosen will be indicated in a dark grey at the bottom of the main black screen, just above the various clock tabs.

This pretty much covers the Clocks app. You'll have to judge whether or not it's better than its predecessor YouTube, which as most of you know had been with iOS from the beginning of the first iPhone. If you don't think it makes the grade, don't lose heart because, as I'm sure you know or will shortly find out, there will be YouTube replacement apps in the future as well as browser accessibility at http://YouTube.com.

CHAPTER 19

Notes

The Notes Application

A fairly stripped down but basic sticky note app, the Notes app fills a void between "Reminders" and a full fledged text editor or word processor, whatever your preference. There come times in all of our days when we just can't trust a tidbit of information to memory but it doesn't quite justify a scheduled reminder. For this task, Apple has given us Notes.

Very straightforward to use in iOS 6.x, you open the app, tap the screen to bring up the keyboard, and simply start typing. When you've entered your information, you can simply tap the plus (+) sign and go onto other notes. Tap the action button (the right facing arrow coming out of a box) at the bottom of your screen to email it, message it, print it, or copy it, or tap the little trash can to delete it.

Notes are time and date stamped by default. Existing notes can be accessed from tapping the "Notes" button on the upper left portion of your screen. They are named after the first line of text you entered, and they can be edited at any time by selecting them and tapping the page in the place you'd like to correct or change. If you want to edit the last note you created, you can tap the right arrow at the bottom of the page. To navigate to the next note again, tap the left arrow.

That basically covers the "Notes" app. In the "More Apps" chapter, there are several excellent note taking apps that I recommend highly. I don't know about you, but I know my honey do list is much too lengthy to trust to memory, so a good, full featured, note app is crucial! I'll say the best part of any iPad note app is that you don't have to worry about wasting paper if you mess up!

CHAPTER 20

Camera

Two for the Price of One

Differences

Now we come to the major difference between the various iterations of the iPad. Of course, the iPad 1 had no camera. The iPad 2 had two cameras a 0.7 megapixel (Mp) rear facing camera with a 5x digital zoom - the digital zoom only works with the rear-facing camera and only in still mode. It also is not nearly as strong as a digital camera's optical zoom but it's not too shabby - and a front facing VGA camera. In comparison, the iPad 3, 4, and Mini have increased from 720p stills to 1080p HD stills. The rear-facing camera is now 5Mp while retaining the 5x digital zoom. Additionally, the front-facing camera is

1.2Mp and all retain the 30fps (frames per second) video camera. These improvements, especially as viewed on the new 2048x1536 retina display, add up to a significant difference.

The app itself has not changed that much between iPad versions or iOS updates so, other than the above listed physical changes, what we discuss here on out in this chapter and the other photo related chapters, applies pretty much equally to iPad models since the original iPad. As quickly as Apple has been rolling out iPad models, who knows what it will be like six months down the road. Let's take a closer look at the Camera app as it is as of the writing of this book, on the iPad 2, 3, 4, and Mini, with iOS 6.x.

Upon opening the app for the first time, you will be asked if you want to allow the app to use your location information. If you approve this, your photos will have geo-location enabled. What this does is provides map positioning in your Maps app, on Facebook, or anywhere else you may post the photo, indicating where, exactly, the photo was taken. More and more digital cameras are being manufactured with this feature. Additionally, there are, what's known as, Eye-Fi cards that replace your SD card in your digital camera, and have this feature built in. Eye-Fi cards are relatively new in the past couple of years and are very handy, especially if you take a lot of pictures at various times. These cards, as I say, go into your digital camera in place of the SD memory card and can be programmed to upload your photos, as soon as they're taken, to whatever location you choose. I generally set mine to upload to my iPad, the Wi-Fi is built right into these cards so, even if you are not within a location that has Wi-Fi, these cards can still perform as programmed. I then set my iPad up with PhotoStream, a feature we'll be covering in more detail when we get into the Photo app, so that the photos are automatically on my iPhone, Mac, and iPod Touch as well as my iPad. Not all of these cards have the geotagging ability as there are different versions, but the one I have for my husband's digital camera does, since his does not have the feature built into the unit. Mine, on the other hand do, so I use basic Eye-Fi cards for those. The nice thing about these cards, aside from the fact that they're extremely convenient, is that they're also virtually bottomless as you can have them delete photos after a certain size limit has been reached. It'll delete the oldest first until it gets to the available size you've set for it. They basically eliminate the need for an Apple Connector or 5-in-1 Connection kit.

Before I drift too far off topic, let me pull myself back in. You will have the option of allowing or not allowing your Camera app to geo-tag your photos by using location services. Should you allow it and later change your mind, you can access the setting again in Settings -> Privacy -> Location Services -> Camera and disable it there. The opposite also holds true, too, of course.

What You See

Once you're into the app itself, you'll see a very basic page with several icons (see Figure 4). On the bottom of the screen, to the left, will be an "Options" button. To the right of that, second from the right side, at the bottom of the screen, is an image of a camera with a semi-circle around it. That is the "Change Camera Button" as I call it. Tapping this button changes from the front-facing to the rear-facing camera and vice versa. Finally, on the bottom, to the right of that, is a little slider switch with an icon of a still camera on the left and a video camera on the right. To switch between these cameras slide this switch to the desired icon.

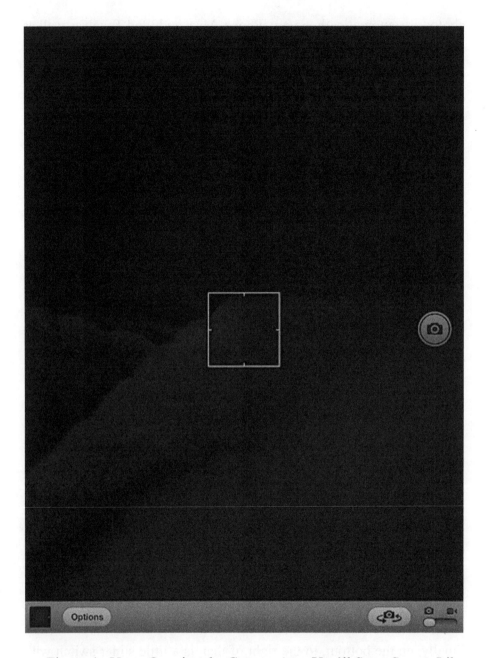

Figure 4 - Upon Opening the Camera App, You'll See a Screen Like the Above.

If you look about half way up the right side of the page, you'll see a little button. Depending on what camera you're using, video or still, the button will look like a grey circle with a red light centered in it, which will flash while it's on, or a grey circle with a camera icon in the middle. This is the shutter button (the one you use to take your photos).

If you're using an iPad third generation, you'll frequently see a hollow square on various parts of the middle of the screen. This is the auto-focus. As you move your iPad around with the camera app open, it will try to get a focused fix on whatever it thinks you'll be photographing.

After you take a photo, you'll also see an image of the photo in the lower left hand corner, to the left of the options button. To view it, just tap it and it will open up to full screen view. One other point, if you have your camera app in the video setting, the options box on the lower left will not be there. That function is only available for still photos.

Selecting the Options button will present you with a Grid option. You can enable it, which will give you a screen similar to Figure 5 so your screen is divided into thirds, to clear the button from the screen select "Done." Some people prefer this type of functionality because it makes it easier for them to center their photo composition. For others, it's distracting and they prefer it off. To turn it off again, slide the button to "Off," then click "Done."

Figure 5 - When the "Options" Button Is Selected It Can Be Enabled Which Divides Your Screen Into Thirds, As Above.

Taking Photos

More Than One Way to Skin a Cat

As I've pointed out, the shutter button is about half way up the right side. For left handed people, this is a very awkward placement. It used to be on the bottom of the screen, in the center but iOS 5.1 changed that. Now, it is not mandatory that this shutter button be used to take the photos. There is another way. If you're left handed, or just prefer to use another method, turn your iPad 180 degrees and, with the volume switch on the left, tap the volume control for a second. You'll see that your picture is taken that way as well, and just as nicely. Of course, righties can keep the volume button on the right to utilize this feature as well.

The same holds true for your video taking. Just tap the volume control again to begin taking videos and tap again when you wish to stop. Many people find this a much easier way to take both photos and videos as, tapping the screen is rather clumsy when you're trying to hold it steady.

Lining Up Your Shot

I mentioned in the prior section that there is an auto-focus setting. You'll also see a center box on the iPad's screen when you're lining up your shot. You'll want to center that box on the central part of your composition. Once you have your image centered, you may choose to zoom in, if you're using the rear-facing, still camera. To do so, just pinch out or double tap in the center of your screen several times, until you've zoomed in to the level you'd like. Double tapping, as I indicated at the beginning of the book, takes practice, so don't get discouraged.

If you tap too often, or too far apart from the last tap, you may actually zoom out. Also, you may already be zoomed in to the fullest extent, in which case your actions will not cause any further zooming to take place.

Again, once your photo is taken, you may choose to immediately view your handiwork by tapping the photo image in the lower left hand corner. Doing so will take you to the Camera Roll which is in the Photos App. So we'll head over there now.

The Photo App

Getting Photos Onto Your iPad

Now Where'd That Picture Come From?

W e've covered the Camera app and getting photos onto your iPad by taking them with the iPad's built-in camera itself. But there are other methods for getting photos onto your iPad for viewing on that great display. In many ways, iPads are perfect picture frames. The size of the original iPads - iPad Mini aside - plus the clarity of the images makes for perfect viewing and enjoyment of many photos.

In addition to actually taking the photos with your device, there are two other primary ways of getting your photos ready for iPad viewing and editing. One we've spoken about briefly, Photo Stream, the other is by importing them from a camera or 5-in-1 connector. We'll discuss each of these methods in a little more detail here and, for the camera and 5-in-1 connector's a little more information will be provided in the Chapter 30 on Peripherals.

Importing Photos

Getting photos onto your iPad from a 5-in-1 or camera connector is fairly straightforward. Once you've done it the first time, I don't think you'll find much to trip you up from there on. You could prove me wrong but, I've got all the faith in the world in you. Remember, there's not much you can do that can't be fixed fairly easily, so don't panic.

I know when you're working with your precious photos, bringing back memories of wonderful times that will never be the same again, it's hard to keep that in mind. But, if you follow these steps and take your time, you should be all set. A simple rule you can follow to be safe is, don't erase your memory card or camera photos until you've disconnected it and verified that your photos are safely in place on your iPad.

To import your photos using this method, follow the below steps:

1. Connect Your Camera Connector/5-in-1 Connector to Your Dock Connector on Your iPad

2. Connect Your Camera via USB or SD Card to the Connector Whichever Is Applicable

3. Unlock Your iPad

4. If Connecting Your Camera via USB - Make Sure It's On and Set To Transfer

5. The Photos App Should Open on Your iPad - Choose Import All or Select the Photos You'd Like to Import

That's all there is to it! See, nothing too earth shattering. If you've followed along I'll bet you're saying, "I didn't need her to tell me that!" But don't say it too loudly, let me believe I'm doing something here and not just talking for the sake of talking, as my husband would think! But that's another story.

Photo Stream, What It Is

We discussed PhotoStream somewhat in the introductory sections of this book so I won't go into a lot of detail here. It has some very good points and, up to iOS 6.0, some very pita (see glossary for a definition of this term) ones. With iOS 6.0 several nice features were introduced impacting the handling of photos in your Photo Stream but, overall, when all is said and done you'll have to be the judge of whether or not to enable it on your devices.

Basically, Photo Stream is a feature which, via iCloud, syncs your imported and taken photos from your iPad, or other iOS 5.0 or later device, with every other iOS 5.0 or later device within the same iCloud account. In other words, when a photo is taken on your iPad, and Photo Stream is enabled, your photos will automatically sync to your computer, if enabled there as well, and all other iDevices on which you have it enabled.

When first introduced, there were some real limitations to its functionality. So much so that I personally did not care for it or recommend it to my students. Now, I think most of those kinks have finally been worked out and it is ready for prime time.

First, let's discuss the limits, Photo Stream will store your last 1,000 photos in Photo Stream for 30 days. After whichever of those comes first, photos will be removed unless your Photo Stream is also connected to your computer. Apple, in its infinite wisdom, has determined that with more storage on your computer, be it PC or Mac, photos can remain in iPhoto on a Mac, or your Pictures directory on your PC, indefinitely whereas, on an iPad, iPhone, or iPod Touch, with limited space available, they should be removed after reaching one of those set limits. Of course, I think the deciding factor in this equation, for Apple, is that Photo Steam photo storage does not count against your 5Gb free storage limit in iCloud. Therefore, the shorter the period of time, and the fewer allowed photos, the more space available for all iCloud users. Not to mention the lower cost for Apple in obtaining and maintaining sufficient storage capacity. OK, so I'm not complaining. Free is free. So it's not a million maybe, but 5Gb is fair enough. It's usually more than sufficient for the average user and, the fact that your Photo Stream photos don't count towards that limit is a really nice feature. So, thank you, Apple.

Getting back to Photo Stream features and limits, at one time, with the initial version of iOS 5.0, you were unable to delete photos on your iPad that were in Photo Stream. This led to many complaints from users and many unhappy, potential iCloud customers. This changed with 5.1.1 but, at that point, it seemed you were unable to delete albums. Now, things have come full circle and all that has been resolved. You can, now, delete photos that are in Photo Stream. You can delete albums. And, Photo Stream has its own section in Photos and enables you to save chosen photos to your camera roll, assuring that photos will remain on your iPad longer than 30 days or 1,000 photos, just not free in iCloud. Don't get me wrong, they can still be backed up to iCloud but, once out of the stream, they count against your 5Gb storage limit as regular image files.

Being able to now save photos from Photo Stream to your device eliminates the concerns about losing your images once your allotted time or number limit has been reached, thus putting to rest most of the concerns that I heard my students and, I, myself had with the early incarnation.

Photo Stream, How to Use It

So, now that you have the history and the ins and outs of it, let's talk about how to use it. Enabling it is a two fold process. First, you need to enable it on your computer, then on your iOS devices. If you have a Mac, go to iPhoto -> Preferences -> Photo Stream and turn it on. It will take a few seconds for it to process then it will ask if you want to add Photo Stream images to Faces.... . Make your selections then close out of iPhoto. Next go to the Apple icon in the menu bar then go to System Preferences -> iCloud -> Photo Stream and make sure that it's checked there. It should be selected by virtue of your enabling it in iPhoto but, if its not, make sure you check the box there. You should be all set with your Mac.

If you have a PC, go to your iCloud control panel in Control Panel and enable Photo Stream there. You should have a folder on your desktop that contains all Photo Stream images. That should be it for your PC.

Now, on your iPad, go to Settings -> General -> iCloud -> Photo Stream and tap the little right facing arrow on the right. Turn on My Photo Stream by sliding the On/Off switch until On shows and is blue.

Then, if you'd also like to share your photos from Photo Stream with others, you can also enable Shared Photo Streams. Back out of it by tapping the iCloud icon on the upper left of that column. Go to Photos & Camera -> My Photo Stream and make sure that it's enabled there. Again, if you choose to share as well, enable that while you're there. If you can't decide if you want to share or not right away, it can be done later. You are now all set! You can repeat this process for any other iOS devices that you want to include in your stream.

As a final point, it is possible to add and delete from Photo Stream now. To add an image on your computer, drag the photo to the applicable folder, i.e. iPhoto, Aperture, Photo Stream. To delete an image from Photo Stream on your iPad, go to your Photo Stream folder and open it. Tap Edit in the upper right corner, select the image you want to delete and tap the red Delete button in the upper left corner. Sharing is handled the same way but, instead of tapping Delete, tap Share and select Photo Stream. You can then share your photos with anyone. Complete the email form, name the photo stream and send it. The recipient will be notified that they've been invited to share. Easy!

Checking Things out!

Dealing With Photos

If you're anything like my average student, if there is such a thing, you've been anxiously awaiting this chapter. Most of my students can't wait to take photos with their iPad, edit them, and put together slide shows. This is, seemingly, one of their favorite topics and one of the most enjoyed classes in a course. So, without further ado, I will begin by giving you an overview of the Photos app.

Upon opening the Photos app for the first time, you'll be taken to the first of several sections, Photos. Depending on what photos exist on your iPad, your choices may differ from these but, conceivably, you could have: Photos; Photo Stream; Albums; Events; and, Places tabs across the top of the page. To the right of those tabs will be a Slideshow button and an Edit button.

While in the Photos section, you should see basically all photos on your device from all sources. They should be ordered by date taken, as indicated in the EXIF data. The EXIF data is the information that comes with every photo, usually indicating the date taken, the size and format of the original image, and, sometimes, the location at which the photo was taken. This information varies with the type of camera used to take the photo and, to a lesser extent, the features of the memory card on which the photo was stored.

We'll discuss the Slideshow and Edit buttons and the Photo Stream tab in their own sections, so let's move on to the next tab which would then be Albums.

Albums

Selecting the Albums tab will bring up, none other than, your Albums. Each album will have its own photo stack with some standard existing albums. Again, this will depend on the source and type of photos you have on your device at the time but, if you have any photos on your iPad, you should have a Camera Roll stack. Additionally, if you've imported any images, as we'll be doing in the next section, you will have a Last Imported and an All Imported album. Finally, you will also have any other albums you've created on your own.

Creating albums is not difficult. To do so, tap the plus (+) icon in the upper left, name the album, save the name, then a page with your photos will pop up. Select the photos you'd like to include in your new album, then tap Done in the upper right corner. If you want to include all of them, there is a button for that in the upper left corner. When selecting photos, a little white checkmark in a blue circle will appear on the chosen photos. After tapping Done, your new album will be created and will appear on your Albums page with its own stack of photos you've just added to it. An important point to remember is that, no matter which photos you move into your albums, they'll always remain on your Camera Roll. That is the mainstay of your Photo app. The only way to get photos off your Camera Roll is to actually delete them from the Roll itself.

To view the images in an album, just tap the album and they should open up into a display. You may have to flick through them to see them all, depending on how many there are. To view one particular image up close, tap the image. You should see an enlarged image in the center of your screen. Once you've brought up an individual image, you can choose to view each photo in the album this way by flicking left to right, or right to left, through the album stack.

When you're through viewing in this fashion, just tap the screen to bring up the controls and you can perform any of the functions that are otherwise available from within the album by selecting the applicable control. Note, across the bottom of the page, you will see a line of small thumbnail images depicting each image in that album. You can select any of those thumbnails to bring up the selected shot. You can also scroll quickly through a large album in this fashion.

While viewing photos individually, you may wish to share one in particular with someone. If you're so inclined, just select the little action button on the upper right side and choose your weapon of choice. Mail, Message, Twitter, Facebook, Photo Stream, your pick. You may also elect to assign a photo to a contact in your Contacts app, Use it as a Wallpaper image, Copy It, or Print it. These are all options available to you. Let's not forget, if you hate the way you look while brushing your teeth, crossing your eyes, and saying cheese, you can opt to delete it, too, by tapping the little trash can on the upper right. Just a reminder, to use the Facebook and Twitter options, you will have to have an applicable account set up and be logged into it in Settings.

If you choose one of your images for a wallpaper, you'll be able to decide between having it on your lock screen, your Home screen, or both. Simply make your selection and set it. Assigning an image to a contact will bring up a list of your contacts. Select the contact to whom you wish to assign the image and save it. We've already covered the Photo Stream option and, basically, the Mail and Message options. Just address the email or message, and the photo selected will be inserted into your message or the photo stream of the person to whom you're sending it.

That leaves us the Print option, so let's talk about that a minute. As promised early on in this book, I'll discuss printing via printing apps in Chapter 28 on Covering Your Apps but, what about native printing to an AirPrint compatible printer. Many printers manufactured since

2010 are now AirPrint compatible which is the format necessary for Apple's iDevices to print natively, or without an added app. If you're not sure whether or not your printer has this functionality, you can check out Apple's support pages where they have a fairly comprehensive list of all AirPrint printers. If your printer is AirPrint capable, and set up correctly, printing from your iPad should not prove to be too difficult. Sometimes those are big "Ifs" but, assuming those conditions are met, select print after tapping the action icon. A Printer Options window should open up. On the Printer line, tap the arrow to the write of the words "Select Printer." Your iPad will briefly "Search" for compatible printers, select one from the list and the Printer Options window will reappear, this time with the Printer line filled in. Select the number of copies and tap "Print." Your photo should be sent to the printer where it'll do its job for you.

I believe that covers Albums. To get back to another Album, tap the name of the album in the upper left corner, then "Albums." Now let's move onto the Events tab.

Events

The Events category generally encompasses dated stacks. If you have a group of photos in an album and the EXIF data indicates they originated on the same date, according to your Apple device, be it a Mac or an iDevice, you have an event. The photos in this category can be handled in a similar fashion to the Album's photos. The basic difference is, to share these photos, you must tap Edit on the upper right. Once that's selected, just choose the photos you'd like to share. As they're selected, they'll appear with a little white checkmark in a blue circle. As soon as a photo is checked, the Share, Delete, Add To, and Cancel buttons are all activated. Tap Share and follow the directions outlined above in photo sharing.

Slideshows, will be covered separately in a few minutes (depending on how fast you read, how interesting this subject is to you, and what else you have to do…OK, sorry again. I've got to stop doing that!). These can also be initiated from within Events. With iOS 5.0, they could only be created from within an Album.

Places

Tapping on the Places tab brings up a map view of the area in which your photos were taken, marked by red pins in the exact locations (see Figure 6). Note, if Location services are not enabled for your Camera app, pins indicating where photos were taken with your iPad will not be there. The first image will be a zoomed out view, pinching out on the pin, or double-tapping it, will zoom in on the area. Zooming in enough will enable you to see the exact street location of the source (see Figure 7). Tapping the pin will bring up a stack of the images taken in that location (see Figure 8). If you tap on the image stack, the stack will open up showing you each of the photos that were taken there (See Figure 9). At the top, the number of photos will be indicated in the center of the page.

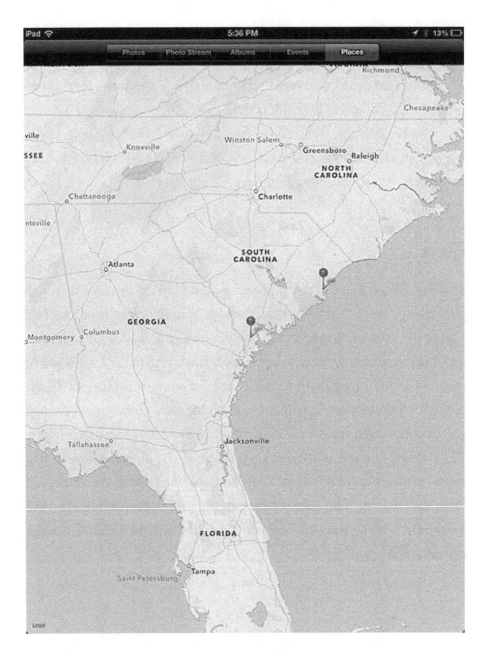

Figure 6 - If Location Services Are Enabled Before a Photo Is Taken, Pins Will Mark the Location on a Map, in the "Places" Section, Indicating the Spot from Which the Picture Was Taken.

Figure 7 - You Can "Zoom" Into a Map Pin Location to See More Precisely Where a Photo Was Taken

Figure 8 - When a Pin Is Tapped in the Places Tab, a Photo "Stack" Appears Holding All the Photos Taken in That Location

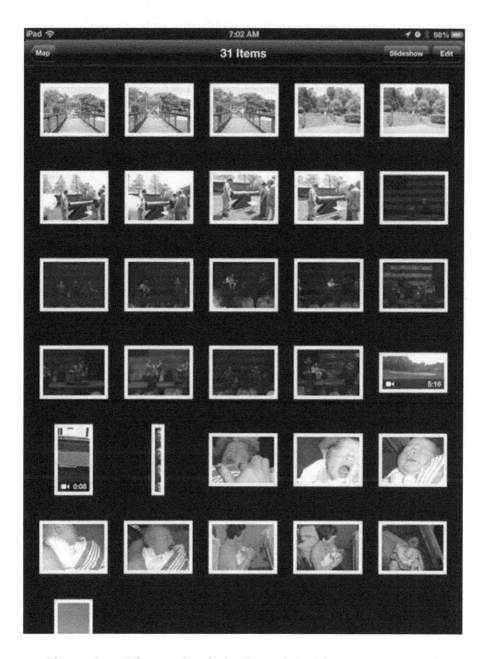

Figure 9 - When a Stack Is Tapped It "Opens" to Reveal All Individual Photos Taken In That Location

You won't be able to delete from within this section but you can still create a slideshow from these images as well as share with the usual options and add them to a new or existing album, like you can in the Albums, Events, Photos, and Photo Stream sections.

Editing Photos

Eye Can Fix That

Although there are limited resources available for editing photos within the Photo app itself, the resources that are available can handle most basic editing jobs you would need.

To access the app's built-in editing tools, select a photo and tap the Edit button on the upper right side of the page. Across the bottom of your image will be four editing function buttons.

The first, from left to right, is Rotate. Tapping Rotate will turn your photo 90 degrees in a counter-clockwise direction. You can continue tapping this button until you are satisfied with the direction in which your image is situated.

On the upper left, will be an Undo and a Redo button. These are not generally necessary when using the rotation tool as you can continue to rotate until you are back to the position in which you started, in just four taps.

Next comes the Enhance tool. I have to admit, in most cases, you will not see a noticeable improvement to your picture after tapping this button. It is designed to more clearly define your image in many ways, color saturation, contrast, etc. With my bad eyes, and I just had cataract surgery and see better than I have seen since I was a kid, I still can't make out any significant differences between an original image and the same image after this tool has been applied. Maybe you will, who am I to say?! My recommendation is to try it and see what you think. It can't hurt and, as I say, it can be undone if you absolutely hate the results.

The third tool is Red-Eye. When you select this tool, you'll be instructed to select each eye that you want to apply it to. If the object does not have a red-eye, you'll receive a message saying, "Did not find a red-eye to correct." If it does find it after you've pointed it out, it will do its best to remove the red. In my experience, it does as good a job at this as many other photo editing apps, so rack one up for Apple for this.

The fourth and final editing tool is the Crop tool. This is used to delete any extraneous background from your shot that you feel is not relevant to the composition. When you tap this button a grid will form around your object. There will be four visible corner pieces. Select any one of these to slide in and contract the box around your photo. The area inside the circle will be the only area remaining once you hit the Crop button in the upper right corner, so be sure you've got the area covered that you want included. If, by chance, you hit that button before you are really ready, no problem, just tap the Undo button in the upper left.

You'll notice when you crop an image that the image itself becomes larger as it seems to be a photo taken at a closer range. When you've selected the Crop tool, you'll also find that there is an additional button on the bottom named "Constrain." When that button is selected, several image sizes will appear, along with Original and Square. Selecting one of these options will alter the dimensions of your edited photo. If you test it out and are not satisfied, simply tap "Reset" the other button that appears on the bottom of your Crop page. In some cases the sizes of your finished images will be altered to some extent to accommodate your selection. Try them out before saving your final project. One concern I have with this editing is, yes, you can undo all unwanted edits along the way. But the finished product has to be saved over original image, meaning that you no longer have an original, pre-edited photo to fall back on should you, at a later date, decide you wanted something you had cropped out of the edited photo for example. When I work in photo editing programs I never save over my original image, I always Save As and give the edited image a different name, retaining both.

Slideshows

Being Creative Is Fun

Pictures wouldn't be worth very much if we couldn't view and enjoy them. As mentioned, there are several ways to view individual photos, but now you can even create slideshows to be viewed on your iPad, or on a larger screen, from your iPad.

To create a slideshow go to Settings -> Photos and Camera -> Slideshow and select from the options. You can choose to have slides appear for 2, 3, 5, 10, or 20 seconds; you can have the show loop or repeat; and you can have the photos "Shuffle" or come up in an assorted order. You can also turn on either, or both, the Repeat and/or Shuffle options.

When done, go to the Photos app and tap on Slideshow. A drop-down will provide two more options. If you select the Transitions option, you'll have five more options: Dissolve (the Default), Cube, Ripple, Wipe, and my favorite, Origami. If you'd like to add audio turn "Play Music" on by sliding the switch until the On shows in blue, at which point you'll have the additional option of selecting which music from your iPad you'd like to use.

Once you've made all your decisions, you can tap "Start Slideshow." Of course, you don't need all the bells and whistles and can just start a slideshow at any time with the default transition and no audio. Once set-up, you can keep those settings indefinitely. Note, you can start a slideshow from photos in any tab in your Photos app.

Framing Your Photos

To wrap up this section on the Photo app, let me tell you about Picture Frame. You may or may not have noticed on the iPad 2 and later iPads there is a little image of a flower on the bottom of the lock screen, to the right of the unlock slider. Tapping that little image will start up a slideshow of sorts of the photos that you select.

To set up Picture Frame, go to Settings -> Picture Frame and you will see several settings that can be adjusted to suit your mood. You can adjust settings for the transitions that appear, how long the slides appear, and which photos will show in your Picture Frame slideshow.

That's it for Photos. Have a great time working with them and, especially on the third generation and later models. The view is great!

```
┌─────── CHAPTER 22 ───────┐
│                          │
│                          │
│         FaceTime         │
│                          │
└──────────────────────────┘
```

Setting Up Face-to-Face

Overview

I f you've ever heard of, or used, Skype, you'll be familiar with the workings of FaceTime. FaceTime is very much like Skype but dedicated to iOS 5.0, and later, iPhones 4 and later, iPod Touch 4th generation and later, iPad 2 and later, and Macs running OS X 10.6.6 and up. Until Fall 2012, FaceTime could only be used on an iOS device via Wi-Fi, but then the gates opened up. AT&T was first, offering 3G and 4G FaceTime service if you bought into their Share Plans. Without getting into all of the various configurations, because I'm no expert on wireless plans being offered and they change frequently, AT&T's Share plans allowed for you to set up a specified number of devices to use with your main plan and shared data. At first glance, it appeared that you had to pay a certain dollar amount extra for each of those devices, so I don't know how many takers they'll ultimately have. I'm sure these plans will undergo several permutations before this book goes to print, but that was the basic gist of the initial offering. Other carrier's plans offering this feature are in a constant state of flux so check in with your provider from time to time.

Back to FaceTime itself, it is an app that allows you to speak, face-to-face with friends and loved ones who are also on iOS devices or Macs with an iSight camera. Years ago when people spoke about a future with visual voice calls, they probably had no idea it would happen in such short order. Now, in our lifetimes, we have this fabulous option. I can talk to, and be in the same room with, my family and friends in other states, as well as family in Great Britain. That's right, I regularly communicate with an aunt and cousins in London via my iPad, iPhone, iPod Touch, and MacBook Pro. I know, that's one big Apple, what can I say. But, it's so nice to be able to pick up and talk to such distant family in just a moment's notice. FaceTime won't work in all countries, there are some restrictions - so check online to see if the country you want to contact is enabled. Alternatively, don't think it's you if you try to contact someone in another country and can't - it may very well be that that particular country is excluded from the list.

Now I'll tell you how you, too, can do this with your family, whether they be right down the road or thousands of miles away.

The Actual Set Up

The first time you open the FaceTime app, you'll see yourself on camera on the left side of the screen and, on the right, a column asking you to enter your Apple ID or create a new account. Enter your Apple ID or create a new account using the applicable buttons. Select Next.

The next screen will tell you that people will call you using your email address or mobile phone number, if you also have an iPhone. If you have more than one, or have previously set up FaceTime on another device, it will have all of the options listed. You can check one by selecting it, or check them all one-by-one. When you're done, tap Next.

FaceTime will verify your information, then bring up all of your contacts in that same column. At the bottom of the column will be three tabs: Favorites, Recents, and Contacts. By default, the last one, Contacts, will be selected. If you want to add more, tap the little plus (+) sign on the upper right corner and enter the information. If you prefer to work with your Group's Contacts, tap the little "Groups" button on the upper left of that column and select only the group you wish to work with. Selecting All iCloud will select all groups automatically, so if you only want to work with one group in particular, uncheck the All iCloud option. When you're through, select Done. Another option is to Hide All Contacts on that Groups page. We spoke about setting up groups in the Contacts chapter and will discuss it further in Covering Your Apps, later in Chapter 28.

That's basically it for set up. Now you're ready to test it out.

Doing What You Set Out to Do

It Varies

The way in which you make FaceTime calls varies based on what iOS device you're using to make the call. In our instance, from the iPad, FaceTime calls are made through either the Contacts App or the FaceTime App. To make a call, you need to have added the contact you wish to call to your Contacts list and they must have an email address or, if they have an iPhone a phone number, entered.

From FaceTime select the individual's email address. If they're logged into FaceTime, their iPad's FaceTime app will "Ring" alerting them to the fact that you're calling them. You'll hear a light ringing on your end and there will be a bar on the bottom of the screen saying that a call is being placed to the other party and there will be an "End" button to press to disconnect the call. Unless you have a 3G or 4G iPad 2 or later, you will have to have a Wi-Fi signal, as will the other person.

To call from your Contacts app, open Contacts and go to the individual you want to contact via FaceTime. Scroll to the bottom of their listing and tap the FaceTime button. A pop up will display all of the phone numbers and email addresses associated with that particular contact. Select the one you would like to contact them at and, as above, your call will be placed. Once again, they'll need to be logged into FaceTime on their device when you call, or the call won't go through.

Receiving Calls

Generally speaking, receiving calls is a matter of sitting back, relaxing, and answering or ignoring your caller. If you are not using your iPad when the call comes in, you'll access it by sliding the lock screen switch to the right, as though you were accessing your iPad normally. If, on the other hand, you are in the midst of doing something on your iPad, you will get a pop up screen with you on it in real time. You'll have two options, to answer or ignore it. If you answer it, naturally, the call will go through and you'll begin communicating face-to-face with the person on the other end. If you choose to ignore it, they'll get a message saying the call couldn't go through and you'll be spared from talking to that deadbeat that you don't have the time to deal with anyway. OK, so maybe you have a legitimate reason for not answering at the moment, I'm just saying.

Basically, that's it for making and receiving FaceTime calls - now go forth and visit away. But, you say, "What if the call doesn't go through? What do I do then?" We'll discuss some options in the next section so keep reading.

What Do I Do When I Can't Connect?

What Do I Do Now?!

On their site, Apple has several suggestions for just this type of problem. I will list them here:

1. Try turning FaceTime Off and On again. Go to Settings -> FaceTime and toggle the switch.

2. Make sure you are using the correct means of contact for the person whom you are trying to reach, i.e. Correct email or phone number; If an iPhone 4 user - the phone number; If an iPad, iPod Touch, or Mac user - the email address.

3. Make sure each person has an active internet connection. Note, if not on a 3G or 4G iPad with the proper data plan, it must be a Wi-Fi connection.

4. If you're using a router, firewall, or security software that restricts internet access, you must be sure that port forwarding is enabled.

5. Verify that the date and time are set correctly on your iPad.

6. Make sure that the Apple ID you used to register FaceTime with is an email address. If not, you can change it at http://appleid. apple.com.

7. Before anyone can use an email address with their FaceTime account, that email address must be verified to be associated with their Apple ID account. To verify whether or not you are signed in, go to Settings -> FaceTime to check. If not, an email should have been sent to you by Apple - follow the instructions in it to verify your email/account connection.

One or more of those options should get you in business FaceTiming your friends and family - enjoy!

```
  ───── C H A P T E R   2 3 ─────
 ┌──────────────────────────────────────┐
 │                                      │
 │                                      │
 │              Photo Booth             │
 │                                      │
 └──────────────────────────────────────┘
```

Photo Booth the App

If you have not yet experienced the Photo Booth app on your iPad 2 or later model, let's not waste anymore time and delve into it! If you're looking for an app for sheer playfulness, without the bounds of rules, here you'll have more fun than any other place on your device, virtually guaranteed.

Photo Booth, in my opinion, was installed by Apple to provide good clean fun for everyone. Its lack of a complicated user interface, and sheer ease of use are a delight to behold. Just tap the Photo Booth icon on your home screen and you'll be faced with your choice of nine utterly ridiculous options for distorting your target object. You'll see the comical results of two of my photos here. The first, Figure 10 is a kaleidoscope image of none other than me. The second Figure 11 a light tunnel image of me with the front facing camera.

Figure 10 - Kaleidoscope Photo Booth Image of Me.

Figure 11 - Light Tunnel Photo Booth Image of Me.

Just select your desired effect, and the camera app will open focused on your model with your chosen distortion.

Take the picture when you're ready by:

1. Tapping the little camera image at the bottom center of your screen.

2. Your completed image will appear in the lower right corner of the screen. Tap it to open it.

3. From there you can tap and hold then select "Copy" if you'd like to copy and paste it into an existing email, or

4. If you'd like to create an email, tap the action icon at the bottom right side of the page,

5. Select the image,

6. Select "Email" from the options on the left,

7. Address it,

8. Write your message, and

9. Send it off.

10. That's all there is to it.

As you'll see, you can also copy it in this fashion if you'd prefer. The last two options are to delete it or cancel the action and do nothing. The choice is yours. In Figure 12 you'll see an image of the option page that appears once the action icon (right facing arrow) is tapped, and Figure 13 shows an email with two images, one by selecting the email option and the second by copying and pasting into the same email.

Figure 12 - There Are Several Options Available in the Photo Booth App Once the Action Button Is Tapped.

Figure 13 - Image of an Email With Two Images Inserted - One From Selecting the Email Option, the Other From Copying and Pasting Into the Email

As with any photos you take with your iPad 2, 3, 4, or Mini, photos that are not deleted, are stored on your camera roll in the Photos app. As you saw in Chapter 21 on photos, they can then be placed into various photo albums to organize them if you'd like, either way, they remain on your camera roll.

```
 ┌─────── CHAPTER 24 ───────┐
 │                           │
 │                           │
 │          Videos           │
 │                           │
 └───────────────────────────┘
```

Enjoying the View!

Watching movies, TV shows, and imported videos on your iPad is a great experience, especially if you happen to own an iPad 3 or 4 with their retina display. When you're ready to enjoy doing any one of these things, this is where you'll want to go, to the Videos app.

All of your imported videos, even home movies, are stored here, along with all downloaded content from the iTunes store. The only way to get homemade videos or, videos purchased outside of iTunes, onto your iPad is by syncing them through iTunes on your Computer once you have imported them there. Note, videos taken with your iPad will not be stored here, they will be on your Camera Roll in the Photos app, which we discussed a little earlier.

A glance at the Videos app will show that there are two tabs on the top of the page: Movies and TV Shows. In iOS 5.1.1 there were also tabs for Podcasts and iTunes U, one for each. With the introduction of the Podcasts and iTunes U apps, it appears that the iTunes U videos will now be viewed from within that app. Podcasts, at least temporarily, will remain in Videos with its own tab at the top of the page, alongside the other two.

The number and names of the tabs at the top of the page will, however, vary based upon your video content. Once you are done viewing video content on your iPad, in order to save space, there are two ways to remove it. We've discussed the one by which you would deselect it in iTunes on your computer and sync again. The second is to tap the Edit button on the upper right of the Videos page. A little white "x" in a black circle will appear on the upper left corner of your video content. To delete it from your device, tap the little "x." This will not remove it from your iTunes library, just your device, making room for more videos.

To view any of your content, just tap to select it and tap the right facing arrow in a circle on the right side of the window. To pause it, tap the double vertical parallel lines at the center bottom of the video. To fast forward, or rewind, tap the respective arrow to the right or left of the parallels. When you are done, tap the Done button on the upper left. Note, you may need to tap the screen to have the controls appear.

When you tap the screen, you'll also see a scrubber bar, like you did in the Music app. This functions exactly the same as it did in that app. You can move to a particular point in the video by sliding the dot on that line to the right or left. You'll see the total remaining time left in the video on the right of the bar and the total played time on the left. Under the video controls, you'll see a volume bar. You can adjust the volume of the video by the side switch or by moving that dot to the right or left on that volume bar.

Basically that's it. Each of the tabs at the top will function similarly, only the content will differ. To purchase content, see Chapter 14 on the iTunes app.

CHAPTER 25

The App Store

What More Could I Want?!

Now Let's See What I Can Do With My iPad!

T hey say variety is the spice of life. If that's true, iOS devices are about as spicy as you can get. With over 500,000 apps available in the App Store, you can take care of just about any itch you might have. If it's legal, you can probably get an app from the App Store to do it. That may be a little bit of a stretch but not much of one, I assure you. If you don't believe me, try a search for just about any term and something is bound to come up.

Upon entering the store, you'll think you're in the iTunes store, the similarities are remarkable. Rest assured, you've entered a whole new world. Many of you may be reading this book because you'd like to enjoy your iPad to the fullest extent possible and can't appreciate all the uses for it until you've been told about them. Taking a cruise through the App Store will provide even more functionality.

As I've said many times throughout this book, we'll be discussing several of the more useful, enjoyable, and just nicer apps in another section of this book, so I won't go into the contents of the store here. Suffice it to say, choice reigns supreme.

Let's Have a Look Around

As in the iTunes store, you'll find several category tabs across the top of the screen followed by a search box. Across the top the categories are: All Categories, Books, Business, and More These categories are all encompassing as a brief view of the More tab will illustrate. The All Categories, the first tab on top, displays a slider of featured apps and editor's picks. Under the slider, you'll find New and Noteworthy, a row of categories beginning with the free App of the Week, What's Hot, and a seasonal category such as Fall Fashion, or College Survival Guide. Following the various row titles will be a See All arrow to view all of the applicable apps available in the specified group.

Under the final row, you'll find your Apple ID on the left and a Redeem button on the right to enter any redeem codes you may have. As pointed out previously, this box is for gift card and download card numbers you'd like to redeem.

At the very bottom of the page are five section tabs: Featured, Charts, Genius, Purchased, and Updates. The categories at the top are only available in the Featured section, so let's start at the top.

Books

Going to the Books category is very enlightening. OK, sorry again but sometimes I can't resist. At any rate, a look around here will show that not all apps are books and not all "Books" are apps. This category is a real mishmash, so make sure you know what you're buying before you buy it. Basically, it is the same Books that you were in when you entered this category in the Newsstand Store section, you've just entered from another door.

You'll find that the same holds true of Business and More because, when in the Newsstand Store section, we're basically in the App Store. Since we didn't go into great detail in our chapter on Newsstand, we'll review them here.

Business

The Business category is broken down further into three rows: New, What's Hot, and Paid. The apps in this category cover a variety of functions from Productivity to Finance to Travel and so on. The bottom of the page still shows the aforementioned sections and, under the rows, again you'll see your Apple ID and the Redeem button.

More

The More category runs the gamut from just about every conceivable functionality and then some. I'd like to point out one thing about this category. There are at least two subsections covered in this area that open up to a more specialized listing of classifications once they're selected. Those two subsections are Games and Newsstand.

That covers the categories across the top of the page. Now let's look at the sectional tabs at the bottom.

Charts and More

What Tops the List

Selecting the Charts section at the bottom of the App Store page will bring you to a two column page with Paid - Top Grossing apps on the left and a list of the most frequently downloaded Free apps on the right, both in descending order. If you like to keep up with the Joneses, this is the section for you. It may be that you just have no idea what might be a good app and want to see what's popular, too. Who am I to judge? Anyway, at the bottom of the columns will be a See All arrow that will enable you to see the complete list, if you want to go that far down in popularity. Just saying.

Genius

The Genius section in the App Store is very similar in functionality to the Genius Playlist feature in the Music app. You'll have to go through some hoops to turn it on initially but, once it's on, it'll make recommendations of apps based on other apps that you have installed on your iPad.

It takes a few minutes for the recommendations to process and appear but, when they do, they're each in their own box insert with information about them and a Not Interested option button at the bottom of each. Looking at one of the suggested applications you will see, at the top, the app that the recommendation is based on, the app's icon and title, the user review ratings, the price, and a screen shot of the open app.

All together there will be 48, count them 48 - not 50, recommendations. At the time of this writing, I don't believe all the bugs have been worked out of this feature in iOS 6.0, as I couldn't get my recommendations to update after selecting several of them for installation and Not Interested. I'm sure by the time you read this, Apple will have these technicalities straightened out and, very likely, as you make choices, your list will update itself continuously.

Purchased

This section is very much like the purchased section in the iTunes Store. There will be two columns and they will be broken down into either All purchased apps or purchased apps Not On This iPad. There will be the familiar search box at the upper right of the page and the iPad Apps button on the upper left which will take you into a listing of either all iPad Apps or iPhone Apps. For additional information on how this section is laid out, see our Purchased section in Chapter 14 on iTunes.

Updates

This section more or less speaks for itself. Here you will find a listing of all apps on your device that have Updates available. To update them, simply tap the update button on the right of the app listing. To update all your apps that can be updated, simply select the Update All button on the upper right of the page.

Discussed for iOS 6.0, was a new "feature" that would not require users to enter their Apple ID to initiate free updates or to install free apps. That would be a nice, as well as a long overdue, feature. This wraps up the App Store chapter as well as Part 2 on Built In Apps. On to the next chapter.

PART THREE

iPad Third Generation
and Later

CHAPTER 26

Features of the
Third Generation and Later iPads

Overview

What Apple's Third Generation and Later Offers

Aside from the wonderful retina display and improved camera and processor that we discussed briefly early in this book, the iPads since Apple's third generation iPad have had a few other nice features to offer. Dictation was a nice feature, the 4G models offered a Personal Hot Spot option and, of course, with iOS 6.0 came Siri.

We'll discuss each of these features separately in this chapter. Other features have been discussed as we journeyed through this publication. As I've stated in my Grandma Talks Tech blog, at http:// GrandmaTalksTech.com, several times in recent months, Apple will release an iPad 7 as I like to call it, more commonly referred to as an iPad Mini, before the end of 2012. Also slated for release at this time is an iPad 4 with an improved processor and graphics.

What can we expect in these future iterations? One thing I'd like to see is the incorporation of Haptic System Technologies, which I also wrote a Grandma Talks Tech blog about in September 2012. What this technology can do for touchscreen devices is mind boggling. It involves creating E-Sense Haptic Feedback using Coulomb's force, a force similar to that created when a balloon rubbed against your hair sticks to a wall. Using E-Sense Haptic Feedback, it's possible to trick the fingers into "feeling" the sensation of touch. This can be utilized in mobile devices by creating high-voltage electric fields which run in a grid and are then embedded across a screen's surface in the manufacturing process.

By turning this field off and on between certain frequencies that the hand is sensitive to, the hand can actually feel surface changes, vibrations, and a variety of other sensations. This could be incorporated into mobile devices in the form on an on-screen keyboard, for example, where users would "feel" the keys and their respective responses to the touch. The application of this type of technology could be far reaching, even beyond the scope of current expectations.

This technology is available today, waiting for touchscreen device manufacturers to utilize it. There are companies waiting in the wings to implement exactly this type of design. Whether Apple decides to develop it further or leaves it to its competitors remains to be seen but, my hope is, that an iDevice will feature this type of high tech in its line of technologically advanced mobile devices, continuing their domination in the field and remaining the forward thinking innovators they have become.

Siri

Sometimes Frustration, Sometimes Gratitude

Once you experience Siri, your new digital personal assistant on your iPad third generation or newer model, you'll understand the title of this section very clearly. In working with her, I've sometimes been at the point of pulling my hair out and, at others, been grateful that she's available at the touch of a button. One thing I can tell you for sure is, like us, she gets better with age and/or experience.

It takes a short time for Siri to become accustomed to your voice, your inflections, and your style of doing things but, once she does, watch out! Since iOS 6.0, she has become a much more diversified assistant than she was in her early days of iPhone 4S only occupation. Now, as she becomes integrated with the iPad 3 and up, she can do so much more than she used to be able to do and, hopefully, with fewer problems figuring out what you mean.

If you've never thought about it before, realize that these "Creatures" have to not only hear what you're saying but also understand you and context in which you are making your request for information or assistance. There are many people I know, some in their senior years, that still don't know how to really listen, let alone comprehend what you are saying (of those, there are few that even care!). The fact that this ability has been digitally created in such a relatively short period of time boggles my mind. As a kid, growing up, I never thought I'd see this kind of advancement in technology in my lifetime! Again, it never fails to amaze me.

Getting back to Siri, let's look at what she can actually do. She can:

◆ Open Apps

◆ Tell you the date and time

◆ Tell you the weather in your desired location

◆ Make dinner reservations for you at your favorite restaurant

◆ Purchase tickets to the movie you've been dying to see after providing you with all the information you'll need to make an informed decision.

◆ Keep you up to date on your favorite sports team scores and standings

This is just the tip of the iceberg. And, with iOS 6.1 she can take care of ticketing at a movie theater for you. As she develops further, we can expect to get so much more out of her. For now, let's be satisfied with these feats and discuss them each briefly.

Opening Apps

First of all, to invoke Siri's magical powers, tap and hold the Home button for a few seconds. The first time doing so, several command possibilities will appear on your screen with a message about how to utilize her features and an image of a microphone. To open an app tap the microphone and simply say, "Open App-name" where "App-name" is replaced by the actual name of the app. Sometimes she will have trouble understanding you when you start out. You'll get frustrated sometimes but, I believe, eventually she catches on.

You can also go to an app by saying "Mail Name," where "Mail" is the name of the app or function from within the app and "Name" is replaced with the recipient's actual name. She will ask what you'd like to say. Dictate your email. When done she will show you the text of the message and ask if you'd like to confirm by giving her permission to send it. To send it, simply respond "Yes" or "Send." To cancel, say "No" or "Cancel." You can edit the text by saying change, she will ask what you'd like to change specifically, answer from among the choices she provides then restate the message. When you're satisfied with the results, you can confirm your request to send it, and that's all there is to it. Having said that, I have to tell you, at first you may have to give her the name of the recipient and/or the message several times before she actually gets it right. Be patient, she should learn.

Other apps work in a similar fashion. You will learn her nuances and, before long, be sailing along the Siri path!

Getting Information

To find out the day, date, time, weather, sports scores, directions, or other details of interest, you will only have to ask. You can say, "What time is it?," "What was the score in the Bills last game?" or "What are the directions from 'here' to 'there'?" where "here" and "there" are replaced with the actual locations. Try not to be too far from the mike when you speak and try to speak and clearly and deliberately as possible to assist her in comprehending. You, and she, will learn as time goes by. Be patient and try not to lose your temper. She doesn't understand. Believe me, I've asked her, "Why don't you know?" only to be told "That's an excellent question. Frankly, I don't know but have been curious about that myself!" And, more than once, I've told her to go jump in the lake only to be told, "I don't know the meaning of 'Go jump in the lake.' Would you like me to look that up?" If you think you were frustrated before, wait until you hear that!

Overall, she's a pretty amazing addition to iPad functionality. When you feel like talking to your iPad 3, or later, expect to hear anything. Even if she doesn't understand you, you'll at least be entertained.

Dictation

Give Me Just the Facts, Ma'am!

With the introduction of iOS 6.0, the Dictation feature on iPads since the third generation almost seems redundant in some apps. In many ways, it's functionality was very similar to the workings of Siri, but was only available for the written medium. Its talents did not extend to apps outside of this domain, making way for Siri.

For what the Dictation feature does, it handles it quite well. I suggest you try sending messages, mail, and other written tasks that either method can handle both ways initially until you can settle in on which you prefer as far as speed and accuracy. You may also find one less frustrating to deal with in this mode than the other. In many ways, I prefer to dictate my correspondence to the Dictation method and leave other duties to Siri, when I'm in an automated mode.

How It Works

Dictation works in a similar fashion to Siri but you must go to the particular app in which you would like to write and tap the mike icon on the keyboard then begin speaking. Of course, to bring up the keyboard, all you have to do is tap the spot in your document that you want to enter your text in and your cursor will appear there. A key difference is you don't have to speak a command first, it won't understand it and will only type it out for you, literally. When you are through dictating, tap the mike icon again, to signal the end, and your text will appear.

In both Siri and Dictation, it is necessary to speak your punctuation if you want to use it. Neither seems capable of interpreting, from your inflections what, or where, punctuation should be placed. If you want to use dictation for any correspondence other than a message or mail or calendar entry and similar built in app functioning, you'll need to use the Dictation feature. Siri won't, for example, enter text in a Pages or QuickOffice document, at least not at the time of this writing.

Personal Hotspot

Putting All Your Devices Online

When I talk about a Personal Hotspot, I'm speaking about the wireless internet sharing available on iPhone 3GS and later and iPad Third Generation Wi-Fi and Cellular Models and later. You may or may not have heard of "Tethering" your device and this works in a similar fashion. What "Tethering" or "Personal Hotspot" sharing does is enable you to provide Wi-Fi capability to your other devices, based on the wireless signal emanating from your iPad. In actuality, this is not much different from your iPad and other internet devices receiving a wireless signal from your router in your home.

In all likelihood, your data plan with your cellular provider is much more expensive than your Wi-Fi service received from your internet service provider at home so, like space on an iPad, your Hotspot availability is at a premium. For this reason, it is usually a closed, or securely protected, signal with a passcode, which is initially provided by your carrier.

Setting Up A Personal Hotspot

The first step involved in setting up your personal hotspot is to have your cellular provider enable it. Generally, the cost involved in doing so is about the same as the cost involved in setting up a Mi-Fi (this will be discussed in more detail in Part 6 on Peripherals) or other type of mobile hot spot. Cost will vary based on your carrier, your plan, and your data usage.

Once your Personal Hotspot plan is enabled by your provider, you can go ahead and set it up. First go to Settings -> Cellular Data and turn it on. Then go down to -> Set Up Personal Hotspot. You'll need to enter some information then submit or "OK" it. Note, once enabled by your cellular provider, this step may be unnecessary. When that's done, you'll be able to access it from Settings -> Personal Hotspot.

When you view the Personal Hotspot setting, you'll see an On/Off switch, slide that so "On" is blue to enable it. A little further down the page, you'll see your Wi-Fi Password. You can change it if you choose to by tapping the little arrow to the right of the password and entering a new one. When you've entered the one you want, tap "Done."

Now, go to the device you'd like to connect to the internet, or otherwise share your signal with, and follow the set up procedures for connecting that particular device to the internet. When it asks for your WEP or WPA, enter your password and that should be it. Both devices will share a signal.

Your Personal Hotspot allows for bluetooth and USB connections as well as Wi-Fi. You cannot use your Wi-Fi connection for Internet connectivity while other devices are using Wi-Fi for Personal Hotspot. According to the Apple web site, as of this writing, you can share only a cellular data connection; you cannot share a Wi-Fi connection, although there would probably be no need for doing so.

For troubleshooting any issues you may have in setting up your Personal Hotspot, you should contact your wireless provider.

PART FOUR
Tips and Tricks

CHAPTER 27

You're the Magician

The Magic Hat

White Rabbits Appear

I f you can't find an item (an email, app, etc.) on your iPad, go to the Search screen by flicking to the left on your "Home" screen and implementing a search from there.

When typing, Auto-Completion is enabled by default, as you type, the software will "Suggest" words. To accept a suggestion, tap the spacebar. To reject it, tap the suggestion. The software will "learn" based on your decisions.

Different keyboards come up based on the app you're currently in. for example, the Safari keyboard has a ".com" key which, when held down, will also allow you to select .net, .edu, .org, etc. options - the Mail App's keyboard has an "@" sign, etc.

In Restrictions, you can put parental or supervisory controls on your iPad. Go to Settings -> General -> Restrictions and Enable Restrictions by tapping the button. You'll be prompted for a restrictions passcode. You can then restrict apps by ratings. You can do the same with Music, Movies, and TV Shows, and Books.

If you want to password protect your iPad for security purposes, go to Settings -> General -> Passcode Lock. Tap the arrow on the right and "Turn Passcode On." You'll be prompted to enter a four digit passcode. To use a longer, more complex code, turn "Simple Passcode" off. You'll then be prompted to enter your existing passcode, then input your new one twice.

If you'd like to wallpaper your home screen and/or your lock screen, You can do so from within the Photo app as illustrated in Chapter 21 on Photos or you can go to Settings -> Brightness & Wallpaper -> Wallpaper - then select which screen you'd like to wallpaper, your lock screen or your home screen. Don't worry if you'd like to do them both the same, you can do so in the next step. Once you've made your choice, choose either Wallpaper for iOS selections, Camera Roll, Photo Stream or any of your albums. The new window will open with photos from which you can select. Select the photo you'd like to use then assign it to your home screen, your lock screen, or both.

PART FIVE

Covering Your Apps

CHAPTER 28

Miscellaneous Apps

Apps Overview

With over 275,000 apps available in Apple's App Store, and approximately 400 owned, reducing this list to a select few noteworthy apps was no small task - no pun intended. Needless to say, this is just a flavor of the what is available out there and you'll, in all likelihood, find many more remarkable apps in various categories. There are also a number of categories that apps can be classified into and, again, restricting this chapter to a small number of them was a herculean effort.

I have included, in this brief summary, some of my favorites in a variety of categories and have attempted to do so with a broad spectrum approach to likability. In other words, I've taken an approach that I've considered to be as all encompassing as possible by taking into consideration opinions from all age categories, personality types, and pocketbooks. Of course, this was not fully possible, but I did so to the extent that I could and have come up with a short list, but a diversified one, of apps that I think many of you will like if you're in the market.

Please read on knowing that this chapter is completely subjective but completed in as fair-minded a fashion as possible. Enjoy and feel free to write me with your favorites. I love to hear from my readers!

Mail, Contacts, Calendars & Everything in Between

First Things First

PrintCentral - Printing App - by EuroSmartz, $8.99 Standard, $9.99 Pro:

I have to start this part with a necessity for those of you without AirPrint printers. The app I use for printing is PrintCentral. According to the software developers, "With this app you can print to all printers via WePrint." WePrint is a small app that may have to be installed on your computer for some printers to work. If so, the makers of PrintCentral provide the WePrint app free of charge for you to install. I've found that many will just work with the app itself, wired or wireless can use this app.

There are other highly rated printing apps out there but I've had the best experience with PrintCentral. I've used it on both of my printers at home, a Brother and an Epson, as well as both of my daughter's wired printers without WePrint. Just sending the documents to her wired printers worked without a hitch.

Grouping Contacts

Mail 2 Group - Fast Email - by YT Developments, Free:

Allows you to create groups directly from your iPad. Many features are disabled with recommendations for in-app purchases but, for the price, it does what it's designed to do. If it did nothing else but create groups and allow you to send email to an entire group, it would be worth the price of admission. There are some additional features included as of this writing but, again, read the reviews, the description, and compare it to similar apps. And, always check the date of the last update to see if there are recent reviews since that update.

Contacts Managing:

Multi Edit - Contacts Manager - by YT Developments, $1.99:

Merges and backs up duplicate contacts quickly, keeps track of contact birthdays with reminders, separates contacts without phone numbers, email, etc. and enables you to quickly remedy those situations. NOTE: As with any contact related app, always pay attention to what you're doing when working with it. Although this app allows you to back up and restore your merged contacts, you don't want to get in a position of having more work to do after fixing things than you had prior to that! **USE CAUTION!**

Mail Clients

Sparrow - by Sparrow SARL $Uncertain:

An iPhone email client that can be adapted to iPad use. It has a simple, straight-forward interface and a unified inbox. Very nice for its basic simplicity. The down-side is it does not currently support push email but, if that's not an issue for you, you may find this is the mail app for you. One more possible downside is, I may have read recently, it will not be supported in the future. If this is the case, you may never see push email and future updates won't be forthcoming. Do your homework. Overall, I like it a lot.

My Honey Do's

The next category of apps seems to be critical to many iPad users, note taking apps. There are several good candidates in this category as well. Some allow for handwritten notes, audio notes, and flexible note taking.

Notability - My favorite is "Notability." It allows for handwritten as well as typewritten, and audio note taking. If you want to take notes during a lecture, for example, record it with notability and take your notes. Later, if you missed a section in your written notes just tap that section and the audio will take you right to the applicable section of audio so you can pick up where you left off. This is a paid app, but the price is very affordable. About $.99 or so.

PenUltimate - Not a bad app for $.99. It provides a handy method for taking quick, short notes. Personally, I don't think you get as big a bang for your buck as you do with Notability, but it is ranked highly by some others.

My Webnote - If you do a lot of online research, you can't beat "My Webnote." With this app you can go to a web page, from within the app, and take notes while viewing the web pages you want to take note of. My Webnote opens a double pane for note taking and is an inexpensive app costing about .99 which, IMHO, comes in very handy. There are many other good audio and written note taking apps, including the iPad's built in Notes app but, if you're looking for something a little more flexible, try one of these out for size.

Variety, The Spice of Life

Notability - When it comes to email fonts, you can feel somewhat restricted but there are apps, such as Notability, which we just spoke about, that enable you to change font face, color, and size or to handwrite an email. Simply type or write your message from within the app and click the action icon at the top of the page and email it. In Notability, you'll see different type faces, font colors and sizes. Additionally, it can save the email as a pdf.

All Fonts - A free app in which you can type email then send it. The down side is that the message is typed on a brownish colored piece of "paper", but you can vary the fonts and the price is right.

Movies, TV, and Video

What's On Now?

Let's talk next about video and movie viewing on the iPad. Images display very well on the 10" screen and the same holds true for videos.

One of the downsides to the iPad is its inability to display flash sites on the internet, although I'm sure Steve Jobs would have disagreed strongly with that assessment. No matter, the situation can be cured with apps, so even this is possible.

Photon - There are several browsers that enable Flash viewing on iOS devices. An excellent one is "Photon." Photon allows you to, not only view Flash media on the internet, but it also is a good all around browser. There are other good Flash playing browsers for the iPad but the reviews are mixed, and my favorite is Photon. This is an inexpensive paid app, costing about $4.99.

ABC player - If you like to watch TV, you shouldn't miss downloading the ABC player app. This free app allows you to watch all your favorite past episodes at your leisure. If you missed an episode of one of your favorites, catch it on your iPad with this app. Most of the networks have their own apps but I especially like the design of the ABC Player.

Crackle - If Movies are more your thing, enjoy "Crackle." If you've never viewed Crackle on your computer or Smart TV, check it out on your iPad. It's a free app that provides free movies. Many of these movies are relatively recent releases, others are old, but not too old, favorites.

Netflix - Netflix is an app you won't be able to do without if you love movie viewing. The app is a free download, but the service is about $7.99 a month for, I believe, unlimited video streaming of many of the latest movie releases.

IMDb - This is another free app that is an acronym for Internet Movie Database. It has all kinds of information about various actors and actresses, movies, and cinema history. You can also find movie clips and current movie showtimes.

YouTube - As I mentioned in the beginning of this book, when iOS 6.0 was introduced, the YouTube app that had become a staple since the first iPhone was released, was gone. As of this writing, I have not found, what I feel is a suitable replacement. I'm sure this is just a matter of time and an even stronger and fully featured YouTube app will eventually be released. I'll keep you posted on my Grandma Talks Tech blog at http:// GrandmaTalksTech.com.

Office Apps

Back to the Old Grind

Office apps are virtually indispensable but there are a variety of them many of which work better with one computer platform or another. Here are two options based on the main two types of operating systems available today.

Pages, Keynote, And Numbers - If you use a mac at home with iWork, you'll find Pages, Keynote, And Numbers on the iPad work seamlessly with your Mac and syncing over iCloud. Each of these iPad apps are sold separately so, if you find you only need a word processor, you'll only need to buy Pages. For presentations you'll want Keynote, and for spreadsheets, you'll want Numbers. They're each $9.99

QuickOffice - If your mainstay is a PC running Windows and Microsoft Office, a very good suite of office apps is QuickOffice. The suite, including Word processor, Presentation Creator, And Spreadsheet app all-in-one, works very well with Office and can be purchased for about $11, or sometimes less on sale.

Reading Apps

Readers are other apps that come in a variety of packaging. There are eBook readers, internet readers, and news and RSS (Really Simple Syndication) feed readers. I'll cover one or two in each of these categories starting with eReaders.

Kindle - One of my favorites is the Kindle. The graphics are clear, bookmarking and highlighting are enabled, searches are possible, you can go to the table of contents and click on the page you want to go to and be immediately taken to it, and the number of books available is astounding, many of which are free or under $4.00. To bring up the controls while reading, tap the screen.

iBooks - An app that, IMHO, should be a built-in app, is iBooks. iBooks, or iBooks 2, at the time of this writing, are the only eBook reader that allows for interactive content to be utilized, in a book or magazine, on an iPad. What this means to you and I is that videos can be viewed from within a book, images can be viewed in 3D with the object in the image actually being turned 360 degrees for full viewing. Again, this is pretty far out stuff we're talking about here. The reader realizes a whole new experience and understanding of a book when they are fully involved in the story in this fashion.

Of course, not all books are interactive, but the ones that are can be something to behold. This, too, is a free app available in the App Store. If you haven't tried it yet, try it now!

Instapaper - My favorite internet or web clip reader is Instapaper. You save your web page from any compatible browser on any of your devices or computers with the click of a button and it's available in Instapaper for anytime reading, even offline. The reading pane in Instapaper is completely clear of web page ads and other distractions

The Onion - A favorite "News" reader of mine is The Onion. A news parody, you can view the latest tongue-in-cheek news, videos, images, and sports with updates up to the minute.

The Poetry App - For lack of a better place to put this, I thought I'd include it here. Not quite a reading app, per se, it is an app that "reads" to you. If you've ever felt like you want to get away from the world, or all this technology, and go back to a less troublesome time, sit by the fireplace, and "listen" to a good poem. This is the app for you.

You're visually taken to a Study with books on each side of a crackling fire. Above the fire are "paintings" that, when tapped, transport you to another place, another time. One even takes you to a universe filled with hot air balloons filled with poets and their bios if you tap them. Other paintings in the room as well as some objects, read poems to you when they are tapped. If your senses are heightened and you are inspired by the scene, one last painting allows you to create your own poetry.

Before I leave readers, don't forget it's easy to read library books on your iPad as well as free Google books. Many library books can be read with the Kindle app now. Those that can't, can be read with the Nook app or Stanza. For Google Books, their free Google eReader is available.

Games

There are some great games available for the iPad, many of which are free. There are also more than a few worth paying for. My recommendations are based on a number of factors and a variety of opinions, coming from any number of sources, my children and, sometimes grandchildren, included.

Angry Birds - First off, I think at the top of most people's list Is Angry Birds. It comes in a number of versions including: Angry Birds Rio; and, Angry Birds Seasons. It also comes in free and paid versions. Often the paid versions are even available free. The main difference is the ads in the free versions. Angry Birds is a favorite across all age categories.

Words With Friends HD - Running a close second, is "Words With Friends HD." This, too, comes in a free and a paid version. It is linked to Facebook and many people join Facebook just to play with their friends. It's along the same principle as Scrabble, with people playing while mobile. You take your turn then go off and do your work or errands. When it's your turn, you'll be "Notified" and you take your turn, then the next person is notified. Game play goes on like this until the game is finished. 20 games can be played simultaneously, if you can handle it!

Scrabble - Of course, we can't overlook the inspiration for "Words With Friends," "Scrabble." The board game has a long history of popularity across age categories and the iPad app shares that popularity. This is a paid app that is, generally, quite expensive for iOS apps. But, at least temporarily, the creators had placed this $9.99 app on special recently for $.99.

War of Words Apocalypse - Finally, at the risk of overtaxing your words, I must mention an app that comes very highly recommended, and that is War of Words Apocalypse. Not only does it come with a very high personal recommendation, but the ratings in the App Store are also very good. I recommend you give it a try if you like word games. Just a note about this, it appears to be a game for two players. It's possible to play against yourself but I could find no option to play against the "computer."

Of course, there are a variety of game genres available, and this is just a small sampling of the number and variety out there, but these three seem to rank at the top of many favorites right now. Don't be limited by the small number of games on this list, as there are many other great games to try!

PART SIX

Taking Things
Into Your Own Hands

CHAPTER 29

Oh, That's What I Do!

Quirky iPads

f your iPad freezes, or acts in an otherwise unusual way, apple recommends you take the following steps:

1. Verify that you've got the latest version of iTunes on your computer.

2. Make sure that you're connecting to your computer using a usb port - Note: don't connect via a:

   a. USB port on your keyboard

   b. USB hub

   c. USB on your monitor

3. Make sure that your iPad is running the latest version of iOS. To check:

    a. On your computer - select your iPad under devices in the left column and go to the summary page. It'll tell you if an update is available.

    b. On your iPad - go to Settings -> General -> Software Update. If one is available it will tell you there how to handle it.

4. If those steps don't work, Apple recommends the following steps, in this order, until you're up and running again:

    a. Recharge - again, use a USB port on your computer, a powered hub, or an electrical outlet. Fully charge it, then see if that took care of the problem. If not, go on to the next step.

    b. Restart it - press and hold the Sleep/Wake button until the power off slider appears. Slide it to power off, wait a few seconds, then power it back up. If it's still misbehaving, press and hold the Home button for six to ten seconds to force close any hung up apps; then repeat the power off steps. If it still doesn't fix the problem, go on to the next step.

    c. Reset it - press and hold the Sleep/Wake button and the Home button at the same time until the Apple logo comes up (about 10 - 15 seconds). When you see the Apple logo, let go of both. When the screen comes back on, your problems should be cleared up; however, there are times when not even a reset will work. A reset should not affect your data or settings in any way the next step, however, may.

d. Remove content - the data you have on your iPad may be causing your problem. It could be: Photos, Contacts, Calendar entries, Songs, Videos, and/or Podcasts. Try removing the data you suspect may be causing your problem first. If the problem persists, try removing all your data by unchecking them in iTunes and syncing without them checked. This will remove your data completely. If your problem is gone, try re-installing your data one category at a time. If your problem recurs, you may have to play around to see which is the offending data. If, after removing your data, your problem persists go on to the next step.

e. Reset settings and content - this is a two-step process.

   i. Reset settings - this step will only delete your settings and shouldn't affect your data. Go to Settings -> General -> Reset -> Reset All Settings. See if this helps, if not go on to next reset step;

   ii. Reset settings and content - *IMPORTANT*, *attempt to backup to iCloud or iTunes on your computer before following this step*. This step will erase everything on your iPad so anything added directly to your iPad since the last sync with your computer will be lost. Go to Settings -> General -> Reset -> Erase all content and settings. Although everything is now gone, technically, you should be able to restore through iTunes up to your last synced condition. But first, check to see if your iPad is now working correctly. If not go on to the next "R."

f. Restore - this can possibly be done one of two ways:

    i. Computer - if you've been syncing with your computer via Wi-Fi or physical connection, connect your iPad and select it under devices. Go to the summary page and click on "Restore." You shouldn't lose anything but the items you've added to your iPad since the last sync and, possibly, some settings. No real harm done with a restore, though.

    ii. iPad - if you've been backing up to iCloud and haven't lost that backup, and have at least iOS 5.0 or greater on your device, you will be asked if you want to "Set Up As New" or "Restore From Backup." Select "Restore From Backup," select the backup to restore from, and follow the on-screen directions. A full restore should address any problems you may have been having but, if it doesn't, go to the final "R."

g. Recovery mode - Apple's final recommended step in their 7 "R" approach is recovery mode.

    i. Disconnect the charge/sync cable from your iPad but leave the other end attached to your computer,

    ii. Turn your iPad completely off by sliding the power off switch and waiting for it to turn off,

    iii. Press and hold the Home button as you connect it - if you see a battery image or a lightning bolt, charge your iPad for about 15 minutes first then go back to step two, otherwise;

iv. Continue holding the Home button until you see the "Connect to iTunes" screen, then release it.

v. Open iTunes on your computer, if it didn't open automatically, and you should now see a message about your iPad being in "Recovery Mode".

vi. Now restore it using the aforementioned instructions.

If none of these things work, you'll probably need professional help with it. Contact Apple or other technical support personnel.

CHAPTER 30

What The Heck
Do You Mean, Jailbreaking?!

My iPad's a Prisoner?

Finally, we get to the big question, "What does 'Jailbreaking' my iPad mean?" Essentially, it's the process of hacking through the iOS - sometimes by creating an entirely new one - to allow your iPad to work with features outside of Apple's preset features and apps. There are always new ways to jailbreak, as iOS updates address and patch previous jailbreak processes, new ones need to be created to "break through" the new patches.

Some people feel that they should be able to do and have whatever they want with their devices and should not be under the control of Apple to decide what those things are. The main benefit is the addition of features and apps, most of which are free, that can be added. The thing to keep in mind, if and when you decide to jailbreak your iPad, is that it voids your warranty.

The right to do so is currently being fought in the courts, believe it or not, as people feel that once they've bought a product it should be theirs to do with as they please - whereas Apple, and some other software and device manufacturers, argue that it is their creation and it isn't legal to mess with their patent, even for private purposes. It's an interesting argument that, if you're interested in freedoms in any way, is worth keeping an eye on in the future to see how it plays out.

As its legality is questionable, we won't be discussing methodology here. But there are relatively easily applied methods of jailbreaking your device as well as, what they claim to be easy, ways to reverse the jailbreak should the need arise. I wanted to merely address the question of jailbreaking as I thought this was something that might be of interest to some of you and that you may be wondering about.

PART SEVEN

Peripherals

```
┌────────── C H A P T E R   3 1 ──────────┐
│                                          │
│                                          │
│              There's Help                │
│                                          │
└──────────────────────────────────────────┘
```

Utilities

What Can This Do For Me?

We're going to briefly discuss peripherals. There are many accessories to complement both the looks and the abilities of the iPad. We'll look at some of the iPad accessories that enhance its usability.

Beam Me Up, Scotty!

Power Packs are handy little accessories to have especially if you use your iPad a lot while on the move. There are two I can recommend. The first is specifically for iOS devices, though not necessarily the iPad, and can handle keeping you're iPad going through a low battery period even if not adding to your charge at the same time. This battery extender is the *Mophie Juice Pack Boost 1500mAh*.

The other is the more powerful *Energizer XP4001 Universal Rechargeable Power Pack*. The Energizer Power Pack is a little bigger and a little heavier but it gets the job done quickly and efficiently. It comes with six tips, none of which is for the iPad, but, generally,included in the cost are two free tips a year for life. The only cost is shipping which amounts to about $3. The tips get out to you quickly. This Power Pack, though bigger, is still very portable and charges two items at once.

Who Needs iCloud When You've Got Your Own?!

The next handy accessory is the *Wi-Drive*. With storage at a premium, and cloud storage requiring internet connections, the *Wi-Drive* comes in like a champ. Bring an extra 16, 32, or 64Gb of storage and wirelessly connect where ever you are, since it has its own built in Wi-Fi. Up to three people can access it simultaneously. You can upload files to it from your computer, via USB, before you leave home and not worry about a HotSpot to access iCloud storage while on the road, just access your files from your own "Cloud."

A Picture Is Worth 1,000 Words

The next peripheral is not necessarily an iPad accessory but it works so well with the iPad that I have to tell you about it here. It's called an *Eye-Fi*, and I mentioned it briefly earlier. It's the size of an SD card and comes with an adapter that enables you to program it using your computer. You use the *Eye-Fi* in your digital or video cameras, in place of the usual SD card, and photos will upload to your iPad from it wirelessly, using its built in Wi-Fi abilities, as they're taken with no need to connect to a computer or get a Camera Connecter unless you want one for other purposes. The uploaded photos or videos will automatically sync with your computer if you've set up Photo Stream or otherwise sync your photos. Once you've programmed it, no other thought has to be given to it.

5 in 1 Camera Connection Kit - The other method of uploading photos that we discussed earlier in this book was Apple's *Camera Connector* or the *5 in 1 Camera Connection Kit.* In Chapter 21 on the Photos app, I explained how these work so just a little note here. I like the *5 in 1 Camera Connection Kit* better than the plain Camera Connector because, for basically the same money, you're also getting an AV cable which enables you to play slideshows and videos on your TV. However, and this is an important but, be careful which one you get as not all are compatible with the iPad third generation, or later, yet.

We've Got Contact, Mission Control

I'd be remiss if I didn't mention this accessory to all you non-3G and 4G users. The built in cellular abilities are great and extremely convenient when you're on the road but, for those of you (us) that can't, or don't want to, spring for the extra $100 or so to get the added functionality, all is not lost. In comes a *Mi-Fi* to the rescue. *Mi-Fi* is the name given to Virgin Mobile's, contract free, version, but other carriers have them by different names and with different packages.

I used the Virgin Mobile model, before I added the Personal Hotspot function via my iPhone. I can give you a brief idea of what that type of plan is all about, but plans are constantly changing so check with your provider before entering into any agreement. I had a Walmart plan. I purchased the *MiFi* at Walmart and would "Top-Up" through purchase of a Walmart top-up card when I was out of "juice" or out of "month." There were three different plan structures at the time I had mine. The first a $9.99 or so plan for so many megabyte a month, the second - the one I would usually get which was plenty - a $19.99 plan for what I believe was 1Gb a month, and an unlimited plan for about $39.99 a month. It wasn't necessary to "Top Up" each month if you didn't choose to but, if you went more than two months without topping up, you would lose your "phone number" and basically have to reactivate. There was no additional charge for this; it was a contract free plan.

What this plan did for me was allowed me, and four others simultaneously, to access the internet where ever I happened to be within Virgin Mobile's coverage area, which was fairly broad. As I said, other carriers have similar devices by their own names and plan structures, so you're not limited to only Virgin Mobile, that's merely one of several options available that may suit your needs. I found it a life saver on long trips, stays where no internet access was available, and long waits in the doctor's office when I wanted to surf the net on my iPad or other devices.

Hear's to You!

Finally, we'll discuss docks and speakers there are a lot of docks and dock/speaker combinations on the market, including Apples own

Docking Station which sells for about $29. That is simply a dock which holds your iPad in portrait mode for charging and/or syncing. Also available are audio docks from iSound, iHome, and Logitech to name a few. Prices range from about $40 to upwards of $100, depending on the manufacturer and features.

Just before Christmas 2011, I bought the **Logitech Speaker Stand for the iPad** and it holds it vertically or horizontally for video viewing. It charges the iPad without the speakers on if you choose or you can use the speakers with or without charging it. It normally sells for $75 but I got it for $49.99, at the time, on sale. It has excellent sound and can be used without being plugged in if you just want to use the speakers and not charge it at the same time. It's light weight and portable and I like it very much. I'm sure other audio docks are just as good, although I haven't seen many that will hold the iPad in landscape and/or portrait positions. Most are just portrait.

Listen to This!

Before I leave this utility peripheral area, I have to tell you about another speaker option that is not necessarily just for iPads but all bluetooth devices. There are several good bluetooth speaker options available on the market right now and you'll find a wide range of pricing in that area. A less expensive option I found, that has excellent sound quality - actually working with your own home sound system - is the Logitech **Wireless Speaker Adapter for Bluetooth Audio Devices**. Just connect via bluetooth to the device which, in turn, connects to your receiver and you have one of the best sound experiences you could possibly want - assuming you like the existing sound system in your home. It pairs easily with any bluetooth device, in this case your iPad and, as you control your audio/video on your iPad you hear it broadcast throughout your sound system. Excellent option for only about $39.

Accessories

This Looks Nice, But What Can It Do For Me?

BeanPad - One of my favorite iPad accessories would have to be the *BeanPad*. The *BeanPad* is a stand which is made of a large round bean bag with an iPad holder attached. It's hard to describe just how effective this is at holding your iPad comfortably on your lap, on a table, or just about anywhere else you could want to stand your iPad for comfortable viewing but, suffice it to say, it just works! This is one accessory I wouldn't be without and enjoy the juxtaposition of its basic simplicity in design next to the very high tech gadgetry of the iPad.

By the way, I do have another iPad lap stand but don't like it nearly as much. It doesn't conform to the shape of your legs like the BeanPad does so tends to tip over, and the iPad is not secured to it like it is with the BeanPad, which has the snap in holder, so it tends to fall off the stand when the stand tips.

Bluetooth Keyboard Case - There are many bluetooth keyboard cases available on the market today, and this is one accessory I'm frequently asked about. At the time of this writing, there is only one very basic one that I have tried and like and that is the ***Poetic Bluetooth Keyboard Case***. That being said, I hasten to add that it is not perfect.

There is one inherent flaw, and that is there is a little bluetooth pairing light cover that comes off almost from the time it ships. In and of itself, it is no big deal. A little well placed glue remedies the situation in short order. The keyboard generally pairs easily with your iPad, the keys, though cramped compared to a laptop keyboard, are not uncomfortable for the size, the keyboard is conveniently removable, and the case is not a bad looking one for the approximately $29 cost. I've spent a lot more and gotten much less. Now that I've said all this, take a look at the next accessory to get more feedback on my personal preferences.

Bluetooth Keyboards - Now that I've told you all about a decent bluetooth keyboard case, I'll tell you my personal preference in bluetooth keyboards in general. I have a case I like very much for all uses (see below RooCASE), and don't care to switch back and forth for different occasions. To avoid doing so, I've found that I actually prefer sticking with my favorite case and using a separate, but portable, bluetooth keyboard.

I am currently checking out several and will keep you updated on my Grandma Talks Tech blog at http://GrandmaTalksTech.com when I've settled on one that stands out from the rest. There are folding keyboards with cases that are extremely portable and can easily be taken along with your iPad while it's in your favorite case. There are also full keyboards with cases that seem very nice, but not quite as portable. The nice feature is they can be used with other bluetooth devices in most instances, and can be left home if you don't want to cart it around with you on a given day. Stay tuned!

Moshi iVisor - Screen Protectors are an important matter that we haven't discussed yet. I believe most device's screens should be protected, be that a camera LCD, an iPhone, or an iPad. The *Moshi iVisor* was designed for the iPad specifically, fits like a glove, does a good job of protecting it, and, unlike most other screen protectors, not only doesn't it leave bubbles, but it's guaranteed not to!

My husband, who hates putting screen protectors on my various electronic devices, actually looks forward to me removing it every so often to wash it so he can re-apply it! OK, maybe that's stretching a point, but try one and you'll see what I'm talking about and, yes, they can be removed for cleaning.

RooCASE Convertible Premium Case - This case is terrific. It has a 24 angle adjustable stand, credit card holders, and a hand strap for comfort in using with your various iPad functions. This is definitely my go to case for everyday use.

RooCASE Capacitive Stylus - My favorite stylus (and, yes, I sometimes use one!) is the RooCASE Stylus. It comes with the audio jack connection string and just fits the hand nice and comfortably. Be sure if you get a stylus, to get one for a capacitive screen, as that's the type of screen on an iPad.

Stylus Holder - The *Everyday Innovations Booksling Pen Holder And Bookmark, Cranberry (BS-Cranberry)* is a band that slips around the front cover of your iPad case and holds your stylus in place very nicely. If you don't have a stylus with the audio jack connector string, or even if you do, this is a nice accessory as it holds your styli and prevents them from swinging in the wind. It actually holds two styli, one at the top and one at the bottom, so if you'd like to carry a pen and a styli, you're in business.

XTreme Universal Speaker/Stand - Not quite as sturdy as some other speaker/stands but one that gets the job done effectively is the *XTreme Universal Speaker/Stand*. Not wireless, requiring you to plug into your audio jack on your iPad/Kindle Fire/Android Tablet or other compatible device it, nonetheless, does not do so in an obtrusive manner. The necessary connection is short and all required cords come with it. A very affordable and basic option worth considering in the speaker/stand category.

APPENDICES
Now What Do You Mean?!

APPENDIX A

Glossary

Action Icon - Little right facing arrow, often coming out of a box. This is generally on the upper right side of your screen or window.

AI (Artificial Intelligence) - Artificial intelligence (AI) is defined as the intelligence of machines as well as the name given to the branch of computer science that aims to create it. Siri is a form of artificial intelligence.

App (Application) - A program or software developed to perform a specific task. Apple's App Store has over 500,000 apps as of Fall 2012.

Hot Spot - A site that offers internet access over a wireless local area network (WLAN) through the use of a router connected by a link to an Internet Service Provider (ISP). Generally using Wi-Fi.

iCloud - Apple's cloud storage. Accessed through cyberspace, it holds back ups of many of your iPad files and makes others available for download so it can be restored to its existing condition should disaster strike. These back ups take place once a day when your iPad is charging, on the lock screen, and accessing the internet. Note: These back ups will only take place if you have set it up to back up to iCloud instead of your computer. See Chapter 5 on syncing and setting up your iPad.

IMAP (***Internet Message Access Protocol***) - A type of incoming mail server that allows for folder creations in your account. It is basically a set of rules, regarding mail delivery, between computers. More complex and fuller featured than the POP3 server.

ISP (***Internet Service Provider***) - The company that provides your Internet service such as EarthLink, AOL, Road Runner.

Pita - Pain in the a—.

POP (Post Office Protocol) - Another type of incoming mail server. A no-frills set of rules between computers. No additional folder creation is possible with this type of server.

RSS (Really Simple Syndication) - A way to distribute headlines and news articles from a particular website through a single channel so individuals don't have to continually check various websites for updates. They add them to their RSS feed and use a feed reader to access all sites they usually monitor manually.

Siri - Apple's iDevices' artificial intelligence (AI) that acts as the user's digital personal assistant. Communicates verbally with the user to process requests for information or assistance.

SMTP (Simple Mail Transfer Protocol) - An outgoing mail setting in which simple rules are provided for the handling of mail from one server to another.

Sync (Synchronization) - The process of merging or copying contacts, photos, music, etc. from your computer to your iPad. Note: The easiest way to get your contacts onto your iPad.

URL (Uniform Resource Locator) - An address on the World Wide Web which points to the specific location of a page or document. It is made up of a specific transfer protocol (i.e., http, ftp, rtc.), a domain name (i.e., GrandmaTalksTech.com), and a specific page (i.e., index.html).

Wi-Fi (Wireless Fidelity) - High speed internet communication without the use of wires. Uses high frequency radio waves for signal transmission.

APPENDIX B

Messaging Shortcuts

IMHO - In My Humble Opinion

LOL - Laughing Out Loud or Lots of Laughs, your preference.

FYI - For Your Information

BTW - By The Way

TY - Thank You

YW - You're Welcome

BRB - Be Right Back

BBS - Be Back in a Second

TTYL - Talk To You Later

POS - Here's one you may find your children and grandchildren using, Parents Over Shoulder

L8R - Later

2 - To, Too, Two

4 - For, Four

DIIK - Darned If I Know

CYAL8R - See You Later

CYE - Check Your Email

CTN - Can't Talk Now

CRS - Can't Remember S—

CRAFT - Can't Remember A Freaking Thing

DIY - Do It Yourself

DYKWUTA - Do You Know What You're Talking About?

And, my personal favorite:

TNTWMP! - Trying Not To Wet My Pants! - OK, so it's not official but I think it comes in handy - especially when laughing uncontrollably!

Admittedly, I could go on forever. Teens have created a language of their own. I guess we baby boomers did the same thing when we were young with pig latin. But I don't remember my parents communicating with the same language. We baby boomers are quite adept at learning these new things and will be fluent before you know it. The only problem is, by the time we're fluent, they'll have moved on to a different language.

What's Next For Grandma

Watch Grandma's Site, http://GrandmaTalksTech.com, for posts every Wednesday, Saturday, and Sunday, and for news about future book releases on:

Androids;
Mac OS X 10.8 Mountain Lion;
And More;
As Well As Future iOS Updates.